Guide to Fish of Narragansett Bay

By Daniel M. Cryan

All Photographs by the Author

First Edition: ©2015

Table of Contents

Author's Note……………………………………………………………………1

Map of Narragansett Bay………………………………………………………2

Part 1-Native Species……………………………………………………………3

    Game Species……………………………………………………………4

    Wrasses……………………………………………………………………8

    Flatfish……………………………………………………………………10

    Cods………………………………………………………………………13

    Drums……………………………………………………………………16

    Sharks and Rays…………………………………………………………18

    Miscellaneous Species…………………………………………………21

    Sculpins…………………………………………………………………29

    Pipefish and Seahorses…………………………………………………31

    Sticklebacks……………………………………………………………33

    Killifish…………………………………………………………………35

    Herrings…………………………………………………………………38

    Baitfish…………………………………………………………………40

Part 2-Tropical Strays…………………………………………………………46

    Jacks……………………………………………………………………47

    Puffers and Boxfishes…………………………………………………51

    Colorful Deep-Bodied Tropicals………………………………………53

    Miscellaneous Tropicals………………………………………………58

    Tropical Baitfish………………………………………………………63

Part 3-Supplemental Photos…………………………………………………65

References………………………………………………………………………86

Author's Note

In August 2007, at the age of 11, I began work on a project to expand and refine my interests in marine science. The idea was to catch and photograph all the indigenous fish species in Narragansett Bay, and write informative pages for each one. I began with a list of 27 species, and established an important rule. I would only include photographs that I had taken, of fish that I had caught.

Over the past seven and a half years, the list has steadily grown to include 60 different species, yet the basic rule has remained the same. In catching these fish, I have visited every corner of the Bay, from the brackish marshes of the Palmer River to the rocky coves of Fort Wetherill. Through these travels, as well as years of research, I've learned a great deal about the piscine inhabitants of Narragansett Bay. With *Guide to Fish of Narragansett Bay*, I hope to pass this knowledge along to the public as a whole.

I have structured the Guide into three major sections, the first of which is entitled "Part 1- Native Species." This part of the Guide contains species profiles for 42 different native fish. To be considered "native" a species must be found in the Bay year round, or regularly migrate into the Bay as an adult. The other 18 species are featured in "Part 2-Tropical Strays." A tropical stray, often known simply as "a tropical," is a juvenile fish native to the South Atlantic or Caribbean that is carried north to Rhode Island in the summer by the Gulf Stream. These young fish survive in the Bay for a few months, before eventually dying from decreasing water temperatures. The line between native and tropical is not exact, and certain species may display characteristics of both, so I have simply sorted each species into the category I deem most appropriate.

Within these two sections, species are again sorted into smaller groups based on shared characteristics. Certain species, such as the drums or killifish, are grouped together if they are closely related or part of a common family. Other species, such as the silverside, anchovy, and sand lance, are the only members of their families regularly found in the Bay, and are instead grouped together by similar functionality. (In this case all three species are baitfish).

Each profile begins with the common name of the species, followed by the scientific name, and other colloquial names. Below the names, there is a color photograph that I have taken showing the fish shortly after it has been captured. To the right of the photo, there is a brief summary of the species' preferred habitat. I continue with a physical description where I discuss typical coloration, morphological characteristics, and average size. In some cases, I include a "Similar Species" section, where I briefly mention another related species that may also be found in the Bay. After the description (or similar species) section is a brief mention of the fish's range outside of Narragansett Bay, followed by the "Behavior" section. Here I discuss a variety of topics including predator-prey interactions, schooling habits, and annual migrations. In the "Relationship to People" section I look at the species' value to recreational and commercial fishermen, as well as aquarists, scientists, etc. In the final section entitled "How to Find It" I describe the best places, times of year, and techniques to go about catching the given species.

"Part 3: Supplemental Photos" contains additional pictures that I have taken portraying various topics mentioned throughout the rest of the Guide. Examples include the distinctive spiky teeth of an Atlantic needlefish, the unique feeding methods of a northern searobin, and surf fishermen angling for striped bass. I have also included a list of references used while researching for the Guide.

Finally I would like to thank everyone at Save the Bay, The Ocean Exploration Trust, and La Salle Academy who has provided support and encouragement along the way. I'd like to thank my parents, especially my Mom, who was always willing to drive me before I had my license. And of course my best friend Tyler, who has been seining with me since the very beginning.

Map of Narragansett Bay

An aerial view of Narragansett Bay. Photo courtesy of TerraMetrics ©2012.

Part 1:
Native Species

Striped Bass -*Morone saxatillis*

Other Names-striper, rockfish, rock bass

Habitat: It is found in a wide variety of habitats. Juveniles often inhabit salt marsh creeks, harbors, and river mouths, while adults live in deeper water with strong currents, such as the surf zone of sandy beaches and deep rocky coves. It also sometimes enters freshwater.

Description: The striped bass is a dark olive green color above, fading to silver on its sides, and a creamy white below. Over this coloration, it has six to nine distinctive horizontal black stripes running from its gills to the base of its caudal fin. The striped bass has a large head, a wide terminal mouth, and fairly large eyes. Its lower jaw protrudes slightly past the upper, and it has small rasping teeth. It has one triangular spiny dorsal fin located in the middle of its body, and one soft rayed dorsal fin farther back, reflected below by a similar anal fin. Its pectoral and pelvic fins are somewhat pointed, and it has a large moderately forked caudal fin. The striped bass's overall body shape is well-built, stout, and somewhat elongated. It averages 1 to 3 feet, and 2 to 15 pounds, but can grow up to 6 feet and nearly 80 pounds. Historically, it grew up to 125 pounds, but fish this size are no longer found.

Similar Species: The white perch (*Morone americanus*), is another member of the temperate bass family also found in brackish areas of the Bay. It is much smaller than the striped bass, growing to only 15 inches, and weighing only 2 pounds. It is deeper and thinner than the striped bass and its two dorsal fins are connected. It is greenish gray on its back and sides and has a white belly.

Range: Outside of Narragansett Bay the striped bass ranges from Nova Scotia to North Florida, and has been introduced elsewhere.

Behavior: In many respects, the striped bass is Narragansett Bay's top piscine predator. It feeds on dozens of species of baitfish, from anchovies and eels, to sculpins and tomcods, as well as lobsters, crabs, isopods, clams, squid, and marine worms. Juvenile striped bass are preyed upon by larger fish and birds of prey, but adults are only vulnerable to large sharks and seals. The striped bass is primarily benthic, although it will often move towards the surface when pursuing prey. Juvenile striped bass often school together for protection, but as they grow larger, they become more solitary. For most of its life, the striped bass is a roamer, traveling around the Bay, searching day and night for different kinds of prey. They can show up nearly anywhere, from rocky coves, to tidal rivers, and even the hea surf off sandy beaches. Striped bass a anadromous and highly migratory. Th arrive in the Bay in late March, spawn d ing the spring, remain throughout the su mer, and move south by late November.

Relationship to People: Than to its tough fighting abilities, large size, a fine table qualities, the striped bass suppo an important recreational fishery over mu of its range. This attention, combined with significant commercial fishery, has led declines in striped bass populations in pa decades. Thankfully, the implementation strict fishery regulations has helped popu tions to rebound, but care must still be tak to ensure this species' future.

How to Find It: The striped bass fairly common in the Bay, and can caught from early spring to late fall, a hough they seem to be most abundant late spring. Angling is the easiest way catch one, and live or artificial bait w both work under most circumstances. It c be caught in nearly any moderately de water, although heavily tidal areas are t most productive.

Game Species

Bluefish - *Pomatomus saltatrix*
Other Names - snapper, skipjack, blue, chopper, tailor

Habitat: It can be found nearly anywhere. Juveniles live close to shore, in estuaries, channels, harbors, eelgrass beds, etc. Larger ones prefer deep, offshore water among rips and currents, but often come inshore to feed.

Description: The bluefish is a bluish green to slate gray color above, fading to a light silver color on its sides, and a silvery white belly. Its fins are the same color as its body, although its pectoral fins are usually darker, and often have a distinctive black mark at their base. The bluefish has a large, deep head, a gently sloping snout, and large eyes. Its lower lip extends past the upper, and its mouth is full of large, conical teeth. It has a short spiny dorsal fin, and a long, tapering soft dorsal fin which extends down most of its body. Its anal fin is similar to the second dorsal fin, however, it is shorter and has a straighter edge. The bluefish has large pointed pectoral fins, pointed pelvic fins, and a deeply forked caudal fin. Its overall body shape is moderately compressed, somewhat elongate, and streamlined. Adult bluefish average 2 feet and 10 pounds, but can reach up to 3½ feet and 25 pounds.

Range: Outside of Narragansett Bay the bluefish ranges from Nova Scotia to Argentina, as well as the eastern Atlantic Ocean, Mediterranean Sea, Indian Ocean, and southwestern Pacific Ocean.

Behavior: Although the striped bass may be Narragansett Bay's top piscine predator, the bluefish is certainly the most ferocious. It readily feeds on a variety of crustaceans, marine worms, and especially smaller fish. It is a versatile predator and will target not only pelagic species like alewives and silversides, but also benthic species such as cunner and scup. Bluefish are cooperative hunters, and will often work together in large groups to attack schools of baitfish. When prey is in abundance, bluefish have even been known to gorge themselves until full, and then regurgitate so that they can continue feeding. Juvenile bluefish, appropriately called "snappers," are just as bold, and are often found patrolling the protected waters of harbors, eelgrass beds, and salt ponds. Adults tend to be found offshore in deeper water, among strong currents where baitfish congregate, but will often follow prey into shallower water. Although juveniles are at risk from species like striped bass and summer flounder, the only real threats to adults are large sharks and marine mammals. Bluefish are migratory, arriving in Narragansett Bay in mid-April, reaching peak abundance by early fall, and migrating south in November.

Relationship to People: In Narragansett Bay, the bluefish is popular with all kinds of recreational fisherman, from the experienced sportsman wanting a battle, to the novice simply searching for a tasty meal. Every autumn, local fishermen eagerly await the opportunity to catch adult bluefish, as they move inshore to feed during the annual "bluefish runs." This species also supports a moderate commercial fishery, and like the striped bass, its populations are healthy.

How to Find It: The bluefish is rather common in Narragansett Bay, and can be caught in several different ways. Juveniles are often found, starting midsummer, in harbors, salt ponds, and other protected areas. They can be easily caught with a seine net, or by angling with light artificial lures. Adults are typically found offshore in deeper water, but can be caught near shore during an early autumn bluefish run. They require heavier tackle, and can be caught on large artificial poppers and live fish baits.

Scup - *Stenotomus chrysops*

Other Names-porgy, northern porgy

Habitat: It is typically found in moderately deep water, over sandy or muddy bottoms, in the vicinity of structures such as rock piles, jetties, or reefs; juveniles are sometimes found in shallow eelgrass beds.

Description: The scup is a dull silvery color overall, darker on top, fading to a light white below, with iridescent purplish gold hues over most of its body. It has a series of 12-15 light blue stripes running horizontally along its body, which fade as the fish matures; it occasionally has darker mottling as well. Its fins are a dusky grayish color often bordered with light blue markings. The scup has a steep, angular head profile, large eyes and a small terminal mouth with large horse-like teeth. It has one moderately high, long dorsal fin, and a shorter, lower anal fin. Its pectoral fins are large and pointed, as are its pelvic fins, and its caudal fin is deeply concave. The scup has an extremely deep, disk-like body shape and is horizontally compressed. Scup are medium-sized fish, averaging 10 to 16 inches and 1 to 2 pounds, although they have been known to grow as large as 4 pounds, 9 ounces.

Range: Outside of Narragansett Bay the scup can be found from Nova Scotia to Cape Hatteras, although it is most common in southern New England and the Middle Atlantic states.

Behavior: Despite its smaller size, the scup is still an active predator, and will target a wide variety of marine invertebrates, including crabs, amphipods, mollusks, marine worms, and barnacles, as well as fish eggs and fry. Juvenile scup are heavily preyed on by a variety of predators, including summer flounder, weakfish, and black sea bass, while adults are prey for larger species such as cod, striped bass, and coastal sharks. For protection, they tend to travel together in loose schools of similarly-sized fish. The scup is a benthic species, and spends most of its time patrolling over mud or sand bottoms searching for food hidden amongst the sediment. Although they prefer a smooth bottom, scup are often found in the vicinity of structures such as jetties, rock piles, and wrecks. They tend to live in moderately deep water, (even juveniles are not particularly common inshore), and cannot tolerate water colder than 45°F. As such, they are only found in the Bay when the water is warmest, from late May until October, and migrate offshore to the deep waters of the continental shelf starting in early November.

Relationship to People: Although they may lack the prestige of more popular species like the striped bass, tauto and summer flounder, the scup is still qu popular amongst recreational fisherma Not only does it bite readily, it puts up strong fight for its size, and makes fine ble fare. The scup also supports a mod commercial fishery over much of its rang and has experienced overfishing in the pa Fortunately, RI populations are now thri ing.

How to Find It: The scup is certain the easiest game species to find in Narr gansett Bay. They are fairly ubiquitous, a can be found nearly everywhere in the u per, middle, and lower Bay. They like mo erately deep water, and are easily caug angling from shore on an outgoing hi tide. Bottom fishing with clam worms squid is the preferred method, although variety of baits will work. Scup are fi caught in early June, are especially abu dant in the middle of summer, and leave October. They can also be viewed by scu diving or snorkeling in deep areas wi submerged structures.

Game Species

Black Sea Bass -*Centropristis striata*

Other Names- sea bass, black bass, blackfish, rockfish

Habitat: It prefers rocky bottoms and areas with structure, such as wrecks, pilings, jetties, oyster reefs, and eelgrass beds. Juveniles are typically found inshore, while adults are found farther offshore in deeper waters.

Description: Like many species of fish, the black sea bass's colors vary widely depending on its age and environment. Adults are typically a bluish black color overall, with partially white scales, and a belly only moderately paler than its sides. They have dark black fins that are often partially striped and edged in white. Juveniles tend to be lighter than adults, a mottled tan color overall, with a prominent horizontal black stripe which fades as the fish gets older. The black sea bass has a large, wide head, high-set eyes, and a large oblique mouth with small prickly teeth. It has one long dorsal fin made up of a characteristic arrangement of attached spines, and a rounded series of soft rays. The pelvic, pectoral, and anal fins are all large and rounded, as is its caudal fin, which often has two extended lobes on the top and bottom. The black sea bass has a moderately stout, oblong body shape, with a slightly arched back. Large males often develop a distinctive hump on their back in front of the dorsal fin. It averages 10-16 inches, and 1-2 pounds, but can grow as large as 10 pounds, ounces.

Range: Outside of Narragansett Bay the black sea bass is found from Maine to Florida as well as the eastern Gulf of Mexico.

Behavior: Like other species of the predominantly tropical grouper family, the black sea bass is a formidable predator. Juveniles feed on a variety of benthic invertebrates, such as shrimps, isopods, and amphipods, while adults target crabs, squid, mollusks, and small fish. The black sea bass, like most other game species, is at risk from a variety of species as a juvenile, but only from large predators like sharks and striped bass as an adult. Mature fish tend to live in moderately deep water over rocky bottoms, often near structures like jetties, wrecks, and pilings. Juveniles are found close to shore, among rocks, oyster reefs, and eelgrass beds. The black sea bass is a largely solitary fish, and adults, especially males, can be quite aggressive and territorial. One interesting trait of the black sea bass is that most individuals are protogynous hermaphrodites. Fish typically begin life as females, and at some point between the ages of 2 and 5, the female reproductive organs become nonfunctional, and the latent male organs become active. Sea bass appear in the Bay in May to spawn, and remain until late November.

Relationship to People: The black sea bass is highly regarded by recreational fisherman, as it is a hard fighter, and has delicious, white flesh. In fact, only the tautog rivals it in table quality. Although the majority of fish are taken by recreational means, the black sea bass also supports a sizable commercial fishery over much of its range. Overfishing has led to a population decline and a general size decrease over time, fortunately the species appears to be slowly recovering.

How to Find It: Although it is not as common as the scup, the black sea bass can still be found throughout the Bay. Angling is certainly the easiest way to catch one, and a variety of live baits like squid, clam worms, and crabs work well. They can be caught from piers or jetties, although the best fishing is from boats in areas with underwater structure. Juveniles can also be caught with a seine net, bait trap, or slurp gun.

Tautog – *Tautoga onitis*

Other Names-blackfish, chinner, rockfish, tog, whitechin

Habitat: It is typically found close to shore in areas with structure and places to hide, such as rocky shores, piers, jetties, eelgrass beds, and areas with an abundance of seaweed.

Description: The tautog's colors vary greatly depending on both the age of the individual, and the environment in which it is found. Males and larger fish are typically darker in color, varying from blackish brown to purplish grey, with bright white chins. Females and smaller fish are generally lighter, and can appear anywhere from olive green to reddish brown in color. All fish have lighter colored bellies, and display some sort of irregular mottled pattern. The tautog has an arched back, sloping head, large human like teeth, and thick fleshy lips. It also has a distinctive scaleless region on its cheeks in front of each gill opening. It has one long continuous dorsal fin, consisting of a soft and spiny portion, large pelvic fins, and rounded pectoral fins. Its anal fin is somewhat rounded, and its caudal fin is truncate and rounded along the tips. The tautog's overall body shape is deep, moderately stout, and well built. It averages 12-18 inches long and a few pounds, but is known to grow over 3 feet long and up to 25 pounds.

Range: Outside of Narragansett Bay the tautog can be found from Nova Scotia to South Carolina, but it is most prominent from Cape Cod to Delaware.

Behavior: The tautog is well known for its almost exclusively invertebrate diet. It uses its blunt teeth and strong jaws to crush the shells of mussels, shrimps, amphipods, mollusks, and several species of crabs. Because they grow relatively large, tautog are generally only preyed upon as juveniles, although sharks will sometimes target adults. Tautog are strictly benthic fish, and spend much of their time slowly foraging along the bottom, often in the intertidal zone. When not feeding, they spend most of their time lying motionless on their sides, either in a rocky hole or amongst marine vegetation. (To an inexperienced aquarist, this lack of movement may be misdiagnosed as a health problem, although it is actually normal behavior). Although tautog are solitary fish, they are not very territorial, and often live in close proximity to one another. They are best known for living amongst rocks and other submerged structures, although they can be found in any kind of habitat that offers suitable cover. Tautog can tolerate low temperatures and are found in the Bay year round, thou they are most abundant in spring and fall.

Relationship to People: Due its primarily crustacean diet, the tautog arguably the best tasting fish found in N ragansett Bay. Recreational anglers lo them because they are easily caught fr shore, and they put up a good fight. Spe fisherman love them because they are slo moving, easy targets. And commercial fis erman love them because they are econom cally lucrative. Consequently, it is no s prise that tautog populations are curren experiencing overfishing.

How to Find It: The tautog is fai common in the Bay, and can be found in variety of different ways. Shore fishing rocky areas, using crabs as bait, is effecti for catching large fish. Small fish can caught with bait traps, hand nets, or sein in shallow vegetated areas, like eelgra beds. They can also be observed by snork ing in shallow areas with rocks or seawee although they can be skittish, so it's i portant to swim slowly, and not star them.

Wrasses

Cunner - *Tautogolabrus adsperus*

Other Names - chogie, bergall, nibbler, chogset, blue perch, sea perch, perch

Habitat: It is typically found in shallow areas with sufficient cover, such as rocky shores, eelgrass beds, kelp beds, and around man-made structures like docks and pilings. Large ones are found in deeper water.

Description: Of all the fish found in Narragansett Bay, the cunner has arguably the widest range of color variations. Individuals differ so greatly, that often times they are mistaken for entirely separate species. A cunner can appear a mottled brown, pale orange, rosy pink, rusty red, or lime-green color, with any combination of blotches and spots, all dependent on the environment in which it is found. Its forehead slopes more gently than that of the tautog, and its lips are thinner. Like the tautog it has one continuous dorsal fin consisting of a soft and spiny-rayed section. Its caudal fin is deeply rounded, as are its pectoral, pelvic, and anal fins. The cunner's overall body shape is similar to the tautog, although it is more elongate, and slightly less stout. It does not grow as large either. Cunner average between 4 and 8 inches, and can occasionally reach 15 inches long. They are usually less than a pound, but can grow to 2½ pounds.

Range: Outside of Narragansett Bay the cunner can be found from Newfoundland to Chesapeake Bay, although it is most common from Maine to Long Island Sound.

Behavior: Despite its rather small size, the cunner is an active feeder, and seemingly always hungry. They are omnivorous scavengers, and will eat barnacles, mollusks, shrimp, crabs, amphipods, smaller fish, eelgrass, and almost any other edible material they encounter. Although cunner often reside in close proximity to one other, they don't actively school together. However, when a food source, such as a freshly cracked clam, is present, cunner will swarm together, and aggressively devour the food until there is nothing left. Cunner are in turn preyed upon by a wide range of predators, including crabs, mantis shrimp, wading birds, and several larger fish species. Like the tautog, they are relatively strong swimmers capable of short bursts of speed, but usually swim at a slow, relaxed pace, and sometimes rest on their sides. As their wide range of colors suggest, cunner are found in a host of different environments, but are particularly common in rocky areas, kelp beds, and eelgrass beds. They are typically found close to shore, but large ones are sometimes found in deep waters around submerged structures. Cunner live in the Bay year-round, are most common in the summer, and lie dormant in the mud during the winter.

Relationship to People: Thanks to the tautog's preeminence as one of Narragansett Bay's top food fish, it smaller cousin the cunner has always been of only secondary importance. It is just as tasty as the tautog, but it is simply not meaty enough to support any significant fishery. They are often caught by recreational anglers fishing for tautog, however, they are usually viewed as annoying bait-stealers. But in the end the cunner is probably lucky. While tautog populations remain unstable, there is no shortage of cunner in the Bay.

How to Find It: The cunner is quite common, and can be found throughout the Bay. Hand nets and seine nets, used in shallow waters around rocks and eelgrass, are usually effective. Bait traps also work, but aren't as fast, and fishing can be productive, if one uses light tackle. But the easiest way to find one, is simply to snorkel through a rocky area, kelp bed, or eelgrass bed.

Flatfish

Summer Flounder - *Paralichthys dentatus*

Other Names - fluke, doormat, left-eyed flounder, northern fluke, flattie

Habitat: It can be found in a wide variety of coastal habitats. It prefers soft sandy bottoms, the edges of eelgrass beds, and areas with structure and currents, like dock pilings, tidal rips, and jetties.

Description: The summer flounder is well known for its ability to change color and blend in with its environment. Consequently, it varies from a tannish gray to a yellowish brown color above, but below it is always a bright white color. On top of this base, there are usually several black and white specks, and all fish have a series of five large ocellated spots arranged in an X pattern. The most distinctive features of the summer flounder are the position of its eyes and mouth. It is a lefteye flounder, (both eyes are on the left side of its body), and it has a large toothy mouth. It has one long continuous dorsal fin running along the length of its body, paralleled on the opposite side by a slightly shorter anal fin. It has a wide, truncate caudal fin, and small pectoral and pelvic fins. Its overall body shape is deep, slightly oblong, and horizontally compressed. The summer flounder grows up to 3 feet and 26 pounds, although it is usually less than 2 feet, and only a few pounds.

Range: Outside of Narragansett Bay the summer flounder can be found from Maine to North Florida.

Behavior: Despite its bizarre appearance, the summer flounder is a fierce, efficient predator. Juveniles feed mainly on crabs, squid, shrimp, mollusks, and worms, while adults primarily consume small fish like silversides, herrings, snapper bluefish, and even its younger cousin, the winter flounder. The summer flounder has two main methods of hunting. The first involves the flounder burying itself in the sand, and ambushing anything that passes by. The second is a more active approach in which the flounder aggressively pursues baitfish towards the surface. Young fluke fall prey to a wide variety of larger predators such as bluefish and striped bass, while the only real threats to adult fish are coastal sharks. The summer flounder spends most of its time on or near the bottom, either resting or searching for food. Summer flounder tend to be found fairly close to shore, over soft, sandy bottoms. They are often seen in and around eelgrass beds, or in areas with strong currents that attract baitfish. Summer flounder are found in Narragansett Bay from May to November, spawn in early fall, and migrate offshore in the winter.

Relationship to People: The summer flounder is well respected by recreational and commercial fishermen alike. Thanks to its delicious, white flesh, the fluke supports one of the most important commercial fisheries in southern New England. These fine table qualities, combined with strong fighting abilities, make fluke a favorite among summertime recreational anglers as well. This attention has had its effect, causing the fluke population to fluctuate throughout the years, making careful management of this species essential.

How to Find It: The summer flounder is fairly common in the Bay, and can be easily caught by angling. June through August is the best time to target them, and the best fishing spots are jetties, sandy beaches, breachways, or any place with a soft bottom and strong currents. The best baits are jigs tipped with strips of fish or squid, drifted along the bottom with the current. Young fluke are sometimes caught close to shore in nets or traps, and can often be seen while snorkeling or scuba diving in eelgrass beds.

Flatfish

Winter Flounder -*Pseudopleuronectes americanus*

Other Names-blackback flounder, right-eyed flounder, lemon sole, mud dab

Habitat: It is found in a wide array of shallow coastal habitats. Young fish are found close to shore in eelgrass beds, salt marshes, estuaries, salt ponds, and most other clean coastal environments. Adults are found in deeper waters over sand or mud bottoms.

Description: Like the summer flounder, the winter flounder possesses the ability to change its color to match its surroundings. As such, its color can vary from a light greenish gray to reddish brown on top, with a bright white on the bottom. In addition it usually has a variable pattern of black and white markings. As is the case with most flounders, the winter flounder's most distinctive features are the position of its eyes and mouth. It is a righteye flounder, (both eyes are on the right side of the body), and its mouth is small and toothless. It has one long, continuous, soft rayed dorsal fin, paralleled on the other side of its body by a slightly shorter anal fin. It has small, rounded pectoral and pelvic fins, and a rounded caudal fin. Its overall body shape is compressed and oval-shaped. The winter flounder is fairly small, averaging about a foot, but can grow as large as 23 inches and up to 7 pounds.

Range: Outside of Narragansett Bay the winter flounder is found from Labrador to Georgia. It is most abundant from the Gulf of Maine to the Chesapeake Bay.

Behavior: Winter flounders are omnivorous and, because of their small mouths, are limited to smaller prey items like, amphipods, worms, mollusks, shrimps, fish eggs, fish fry, and marine algae. They are preyed upon by a wide range of species including birds such as gulls and ospreys, as well as fish like sculpins and searobins. The winter flounder spends most of its time lying stationary on the bottom, but will occasionally move through the intertidal zone in search of food. Although they don't school, juveniles often congregate in areas with strong tidal currents, like breachways or brackish creeks, where they can hide amongst the seaweed and ambush prey. As their name suggests, winter flounder are most common in Narragansett Bay in the winter, when they enter shallow coastal waters to spawn. At this time, adult fish can be found in shallow waters over muddy bottoms. As the water warms, however, adult fish move offshore into deeper, colder waters, leaving the juvenile fish to continue growing. For the rest of the year, juvenile fish can be found in a variety of shallow coastal habitats.

Relationship to People: The winter flounder once supported a valuable commercial and recreational fishery in Narragansett Bay. However, in the late 1980's and early 1990's the population declined dramatically, and a moratorium on fishing was issued. Nowadays, with an increased emphasis on conservation, stocks are beginning to recover, but the fishery is still strictly regulated, and the harvest of winter flounder is prohibited in Narragansett Bay.

How to Find It: The methods used to find winter flounder vary greatly depending on the age of the fish one is targeting. If a person wanted to catch an adult for consumption, the best way to do so is by fishing from March to early May, in shallow protected waters, using sandworms or clams as bait. If one wanted to find a winter flounder simply out of curiosity, juveniles can be found throughout the summer using a variety of methods. They can be caught with nets or bait traps in almost any clean inshore environment. They are also often seen when snorkeling in shallow sandy areas.

Flatfish

Hogchoker - *Trinectes maculatus*
Other Name-American sole, sole, black flatfish, freshwater flounder

Habitat: It is almost always found in brackish water streams, over sand, silt, or mud bottoms.

Description: On one side of its body, the hogchoker is a dusky-brown color with a variety of darker spots, dashes, and stripes. On the other side, it is a dirty white color, sometimes with several dark markings. It has very small scales, and its skin is covered by a layer of thick, slimy mucus. The hogchoker can be easily distinguished by its blunt head lacking any distinct snout, small beady eyes, and tiny, somewhat crooked mouth. It has one long soft dorsal fin which extends from its upper lip to its caudal peduncle, and a slightly rounded caudal fin. Its anal fin extends from its caudal peduncle to its small, rounded pelvic fin, and it is unique among flatfish in that it has no pectoral fins. The hogchoker has a deep, thin, oval-shaped body, with a slightly concave underside. It is significantly smaller than any of the Bay's other flatfish, growing to a maximum of only 6 inches long.

Range: Outside of Narragansett Bay the hogchoker is found from Maine to Panama, including the Gulf of Mexico and parts of the Caribbean. It is also common in many rivers throughout its range.

Behavior: Due to its small size, and even smaller mouth, the hogchoker's diet is restricted to worms and crustaceans, as well as various kinds of algae. It is in turn vulnerable to herons, ospreys, striped bass, blue crabs, and a host of other estuarine predators. Fortunately, it has several means of defense. The hogchoker stays hidden from most predators by spending the majority of its time lying inactive on the bottom, often times partially burying itself in the sediment. Its camouflage is perfectly suited for the sand, silt, or mud bottoms that it calls home, and its low, curved profile allows it to actually stick to the bottom like a suction cup. The hogchoker is also found almost exclusively in the brackish portion of coastal streams and marshes, which are inaccessible to many of the Bay's larger predators. During the summer, adult hogchokers move to the mouth of their local estuary and begin spawning. Once the next generation has hatched, the young hogchokers move upstream to overwinter in the protected freshwater portions of the river. As they grow larger, they begin slowly moving, year by year, towards the mouth of the estuary, until they are eventually mature enough to mate, and begin the cycle again.

Relationship to People: L[ike] most flatfish, the hogchoker is said to ma[ke] fine table fare, although it is so small, t[hat] recreational and commercial anglers alm[ost] never bother targeting them. Its bizarre na[me] "hogchoker" comes from old stories of far[m]ers who fed the fish to their hogs, who h[ad] difficulty swallowing the fish, due to [its] rough scales and numerous small bon[es]. Nowadays, the main use of the hogchoke[r is] in the aquarium trade, where they are of[ten] marketed under the name "freshwater flou[n]der." (This is a misnomer, however, as t[he] hogchoker is a member of the sole fami[ly] and not a true flounder).

How to Find It: The hogchoker is n[ot] particularly common in the Bay, due to [its] strict habitat specifications, although t[his] does make targeting one fairly straightfo[r]ward. They are typically found in the brac[k]ish rivers of the upper Bay, over sand, silt, [or] mud bottoms. They can be caught with ha[nd] nets, although seine nets work best.

Cods

Atlantic Cod - *Gadus morhua*

Other Names - cod, scrod, rock cod, morue

Habitat: It is typically found in deep water over sandy, rocky, or shell-strewn bottoms, sometimes around deep-water wrecks.

Description: The Atlantic cod is certainly one of the most iconic fish in New England. Its overall color varies greatly from grayish green, to brick red, to nearly black, although the belly is always a pale white. Its fins vary in color accordingly, its sides are covered with round, rusty orange spots, and its lateral line is always paler than the rest of its body. The cod has a large sloping head, large eyes, and a blunt conical snout. It has a large, wide mouth with small teeth, and a barbel just below its chin. It has three semi-triangular dorsal fins, the last two of which are mirrored below by similar-shaped anal fins. The pelvic and pectoral fins are both long and pointed, and the caudal fin is wide and broom-shaped. The Atlantic cod is one of the largest fish in Narragansett Bay. Historically it attained sizes over 200 pounds, but today the maximum is around 90 pounds, and the average is 10-20 pounds.

Similar Species: The haddock (*Melanogrammus aeglefinus*) and pollock (*Pollachius virens*) are two other cods also occasionally found in the Bay. They have similar habits to the Atlantic cod, but they're usually found in colder water. The pollock is distinguished by its plain olive green color lacking any spots, and the haddock by its dark lateral line, and black patch above its pectoral fins.

Range: Outside of Narragansett Bay the Atlantic cod is found from Greenland and Baffin Island to Cape Hatteras, and in the Northeastern Atlantic Ocean off Europe.

Behavior: As its large size would suggest, the Atlantic cod is an efficient predator. It feeds on everything from amphipods, copepods and barnacle larvae as a juvenile, to brittle stars, tunicates, crabs, sea urchins, fish and even sea ducks as an adult. Its preferred prey items, however, are mollusks such as clams, cockles, and mussels. Young cod often fall prey to species such as pollock and squid, but adults are only vulnerable to larger species such as sharks, seals, and pilot whales. The cod is primarily a benthic species, and adults are typically found closer to the bottom than juveniles, although they will occasionally move towards the surface in pursuit of prey. Although they do not travel in large schools, cod often move around in small groups, especially while hunting. Cod require cold temperatures between 34 and 46°F, and as such they are generally found in water a few hundred feet deep; juveniles only come towards shore in the winter. In the Bay, cod undergo seasonal migrations and are found in the late fall, winter, and early spring months.

Relationship to People: For centuries, Atlantic cod have supported the most important commercial fishery on the eastern seaboard. Atlantic cod have long been considered an excellent food fish, and are still used today in "fish and chips." Unfortunately, increased fishing pressure in the mid-20th Century has led to a dramatic reduction in cod populations. Strict regulations have been enacted to restore cod stocks, but it will be decades before the population fully recovers.

How to Find It: Finding an Atlantic cod is actually fairly straightforward. In the Bay, they live too deep to catch from shore, or to be seen scuba diving. The only practical option is bottom fishing offshore from a boat, (this is easily done on a party or charter boat), using large clams or jigs as bait.

Cods
Atlantic Tomcod -*Microgadus tomcod*
Other Names-tomcod, tommie, frostfish

Habitat: It typically lives in shallow protected waters, often in estuaries, river mouths, or eelgrass beds, although it is not particularly selective. It also has a high tolerance for freshwater, and is often found far up coastal rivers.

Description: The Atlantic tomcod is a beautiful fish. It is a dark olive green above, fading to a lighter greenish yellow on its sides, and eventually to a yellowish white belly; its fins are typically a reddish bronze color. Over most of its body, the tomcod is mottled with several dark blotches, and along its belly there is often a series of tiny black dots. It has a gently sloping head profile, its eyes are fairly small, and so is its chin barbel. Like other members of the cod family, it has three rounded dorsal fins, the second two of which are reflected below by similarly shaped anal fins. It has a rounded caudal fin, rounded pectoral fins, and distinctively long pelvic fins. Its body shape is similar to that of the Atlantic cod, although it is generally more slender. Compared to other species in the cod family, the tomcod is fairly small, growing no larger than 16 inches and only slightly over a pound.

Range: Outside of Narragansett Bay the Atlantic tomcod is found from Labrador to Virginia. It is also found in freshwater lakes and rivers over much of its range.

Behavior: The Atlantic tomcod is a bottom feeder, and hunts by using its barbel and ventral fins to stir up small marine organisms, like shrimp, amphipods, marine worms, mollusks, squid, and fish fry. They are vulnerable to predation by any fish larger than them, such as pollock, striped bass, and bluefish. The tomcod is a fairly inactive, solitary fish, and spends most of its time resting on the bottom, moving only to search for food. They are almost always found in shallow, protected water in a variety of habitats, especially in eelgrass beds and river mouths. They often ascend freshwater rivers several miles, and there are even some populations landlocked in Canadian lakes. The Atlantic tomcod is a hardy fish, and is known to tolerate extremes in temperature, salinity, and in some cases, pollution. Over the past 60 years, certain populations of tomcod have developed resistance to PCB's, (a type of industrial pollutant), thanks to a genetic mutation, which prevents PCB's from adhering to receptor proteins, and activating harmful genes. They also tolerate cold temperatures and are found during the winter when most other fish are absent. They spawn from November to February, and are one of the first species encountered in the spring.

Relationship to People: Although Atlantic tomcod do not share the same notoriety as their larger relatives, they still bring great enjoyment to recreational anglers. They are too small to be commercially important, although they are still tasty. So in the winter, when other fish are absent, a few tough recreational fishermen brave the cold weather and target them. Fortunately for the species, the fishing pressure is not strong enough to endanger the population.

How to Find It: Atlantic tomcod are fairly common in Narragansett Bay, and there are several options for one trying to catch them. Large fish can be caught during the winter by angling. Light tackle and natural baits such as marine worms, clam, squid, and cut fish, work well when fishing at the mouth of a river. In April or May, smaller fish can be caught in most shallow areas using a bait trap. They can also sometimes be caught while seining in eelgrass beds.

Cods

Red Hake - *Urophycis chuss*

Other Names - squirrel hake, squirrel ling, ling, hake

Habitat: Adults are typically found in the deeper waters of offshore banks, although they can sometimes be found in cold, inshore waters over soft bottoms. Juveniles are often found close to shore, particularly in eelgrass beds.

Description: The red hake is called such because of the reddish brown color on its back and sides, which fades to a bright whitish color on its belly. Its fins are more or less the same color as the rest of its body, except for its pelvic fins which are a pale whitish pink color. The red hake has a fairly large head with a blunt nose, very large eyes, and a terminal mouth with a small chin barbel. Its most distinctive features are its two long, filamentous, forked pelvic fins which extend from the bottom of its gill plate to the origin of its anal fin. The red hake has two soft dorsal fins, the first of which is small and pointed, and the second of which is short, rectangular, and extends along its back to its caudal fin. Its anal fin is similar to the second dorsal fin, and its caudal fin is small and rounded. Its overall body shape is elongated, tapering, and somewhat cylindrical. The red hake grows up to 7 pounds and 30 inches, but averages only 2 or 3 pounds and less than 20 inches.

Similar Species: The white hake (*Urophycis tenuis*) is very similar to the red hake in both behavior and appearance. In fact, the only definite way to distinguish between the two is by counting their scales, although most of the time, white hake are lighter in color than red hake.

Range: Outside of Narragansett Bay the red hake is found from Labrador to Cape Hatteras, North Carolina.

Behavior: The red hake is a bottom feeder, and uses its pelvic fins to search along the sea floor for organisms such as crabs, shrimps, worms, amphipods, squid, and a variety of small fish species. Red hake are in turn preyed upon by larger fish such as summer flounder, striped bass, and cod. The red hake is a fairly sluggish, solitary fish, which spends most of its time resting, or slowly cruising around, stirring up the bottom in search of prey. Juvenile hake often exhibit a unique commensal relationship with sea scallops, in which they live in the mantle cavity of the mollusk for several months, using it as a form of protection until they are large enough to survive on their own. They are also sometimes found in eelgrass beds, where the abundant cover provides shelter from predators. Larger fish, however, do not require such protection, and tend to be found offshore over soft bottoms, in water a few hundred feet deep. Red hake undergo a series of seasonal migrations, staying offshore during the winter, moving inshore in the spring and summer to spawn, and migrating offshore again in the fall.

Relationship to People: Red hake support a minor commercial fishery in southern New England, although they are not aggressively targeted because of their soft meat and poor storage properties. This lack of fishing pressure, along with proper fisheries management, has allowed stocks to remain healthy. Recreational anglers do not usually target hake, but they are often caught by fishermen on deep-sea party boats.

How to Find It: Red hake are not particularly common, although they are sometimes found in the eelgrass beds and deep waters near the mouth of the Bay. Juveniles can occasionally be caught by seining through eelgrass beds, and adults can be caught by bottom fishing with cut-baits from deep-sea party or charter boats.

Drums

Silver Perch - *Bairdiella chrysoura*

Other Names- sand perch, silver croaker, yellowtail, sugar trout, silver trout

Habitat: It is found in shallow coastal waters, typically over sand or mud bottoms, and in protected areas, such as salt marshes, estuaries, bays, and tidal rivers.

Description: The silver perch, as its name suggests, is a dark silvery bronze color above, fading to a light white color around its belly. In addition to this base color, it also has a series of faint dusky stripes running horizontally along its body. Its fins are yellowish orange in color. It has large eyes, a relatively large terminal mouth, and a slightly rounded nose. The silver perch has one triangular spiny dorsal fin, immediately followed by a short semi-triangular soft dorsal fin. Its anal fin is similar to the soft dorsal fin, its pectoral fins are rounded, and its caudal fin is a unique double-truncate shape. The silver perch has a sloping, somewhat arched back, and an oblong, compressed, oval-like body shape. It is a rather small fish, averaging around half a foot in length, and growing no longer than 9 inches.

Similar Species: The Atlantic croaker (*Micropogonias undulatus*), and the spot (*Leiostomus xanthurus*), are two other drum species occasionally found in Narragansett Bay. The Atlantic croaker differs from the silver perch, in that it has a downward pointing mouth, its soft dorsal fin and body shape are more elongated, and it grows to about 2 feet long. The spot has a steeper head profile than the silver perch, and gets its name from its distinctive black shoulder spot, located at the base of a series of diagonal black stripes.

Range: Outside of Narragansett Bay the silver perch is found from southern New England to South Florida, as well as in the Gulf of Mexico to northern Mexico.

Behavior: Because of its rather small size, the silver perch is limited to feeding on small prey items, such as copepods, amphipods, isopods, marine worms, mysid shrimps, and small fishes. Silver perch are in turn preyed upon by larger species of fish, such as striped bass, weakfish, and bluefish. The silver perch is a moderately active fish, spending most of its time foraging near the ocean bottom. They does not actively school, but are often found living in relatively close proximity to one another. The silver perch inhabits a wide array of coastal habitats, especially protected areas over sand or mud bottoms, such as estuaries, bays, harbors and tidal creeks. It is found in Narragansett Bay from June to September, spawns primarily July and August, and migrates south deeper waters in the fall.

Relationship to People: Due to small size and relative scarcity, the sil perch has no great economic value to co mercial fishermen in southern New Engla Farther south, however, where they gr larger and are more plentiful, a small co mercial fishery for silver perch does exi Recreational anglers also occasionally targ silver perch, as they are a delicious pan-fis And where they are more common, they a often used as bait for larger game fish.

How to Find It: The silver perch fairly rare in Narragansett Bay, and findi one is often a matter of luck. To increa one's luck in catching a silver perch, the b places to look are shallow protected are over sandy and muddy bottoms, such as ha bors, estuaries and salt marsh creeks. In t Mid-Atlantic and Gulf States, they can caught by angling with extremely light tack from docks or piers, however, in Narraga sett Bay, the best way of catching them with a seine net or a bait trap.

Drums

Northern Kingfish - *Menticirrhus saxatillis*

Other Names - kingfish, northern whiting, sea mullet, kingcroaker

Habitat: It typically lives in shallow to moderately deep water over hard sandy bottoms. It likes areas with tidal currents, and is often found within the surf zone of sandy beaches.

Description: The northern kingfish can be any shade of gray or tan on its back and sides, but is always a creamy white on its belly. It has several dark blotches running horizontally across its body, a series of dark vertical cross bars, and a distinctive V-shaped saddle located just below its first dorsal fin. Its fins are a dusky brown color, and the bottom half of its caudal fin is typically black. It has a distinctive head, with large eyes and nostrils, and a blunt snout. Its mouth points downward and it has a small fleshy barbel located on its lower lip. The northern kingfish has a triangular spiny dorsal fin with a filamentous third ray, and an elongated soft dorsal fin. Its pectoral, pelvic, and anal fins are all fairly rounded. The kingfish also has a unique caudal fin that is rounded on the lower half and concave on the upper half. Its body is elongated and somewhat fusiform in shape, and it has a slight hump in its back with a gently sloping head profile. The northern kingfish can grow to 18 inches long and over two pounds, but averages between 6 and 12 inches long and under half a pound.

Range: Outside of Narragansett Bay the northern kingfish is found from Massachusetts to South Florida. It is also found in the Gulf of Mexico to the Yucatan Peninsula.

Behavior: The northern kingfish is a strict bottom feeder and uses its sensitive chin barbel to detect prey hiding on or just beneath the ocean floor. It feeds on worms, crabs, mollusks, small fish, and especially shrimp. Kingfish are in turn vulnerable to larger species of fish such as striped bass and bluefish. The northern kingfish is a fairly active species, and spends its days schooling near the bottom in search of food. They move with the currents, often coming close to shore, even into the wash zone when the tide is at its highest. And as the tide recedes, they follow it once again to the shelter of deeper water. The northern kingfish is usually found over hard sandy bottoms and is attracted to areas with currents, such as the surf zone of beaches. It is primarily a summer fish, and is found in Narragansett Bay from late May through September. Kingfish spawn from April through August, although because the Bay is in the northern part of their range, the fish here do not spawn until mid-summer. Unlike other drums, the kingfish does not produce any vocal sounds.

Relationship to People: Thanks to its relatively small size, the northern kingfish is of little value to commercial fisherman. It is, however, quite popular amongst recreational surf fishermen, especially in the Mid-Atlantic States where it grows the largest. Kingfish not only bite readily on most baits, they also put up a strong fight for their size, and make delicious table fare.

How to Find It: The northern kingfish is uncommon in Narragansett Bay, and can be difficult to target. The best places to look for them are sandy coves and beaches with currents or strong tides, although in Narragansett Bay, populations are typically local, and kingfish will simply be absent in some locations. The most effective method of catching them is by fishing in the surf, using small hooks baited with cut squid or clam worms. Juveniles are also sometimes caught while seining over sandy bottoms, although they move quickly and can be tough to trap.

Sharks and Rays

Little Skate *-Raja erinacea*

Other Names-common skate, skate, raja

Habitat: It is generally found over sandy bottoms in moderately deep water, although it will move into shallower waters at high tide. It is sometimes found on the outer edges of eelgrass beds, and prefers areas of high salinity.

Description: Many people consider the little skate to be the ugliest fish found in the Bay, and as such, it is quite recognizable. Its overall color is a light tannish brown on top, and a creamy white on the bottom. Over this background, it has several variably sized black spots, which differ depending on its surroundings. A series of small, sharp spikes cover its entire body, especially its tail. On top of its body, the skate has two small eyes located slightly forward of two circular gill openings called spiracles. These spiracles filter water to a set of gills located on its underside, directly behind a mouth filled with a series of plate-like teeth. The little skate has two soft dorsal fins located far back on its tail, and unlike most other fish which have two pectoral fins on each side of the body, the skate has two wide, triangular "wings". Its overall body shape is wide, flattened, and triangular, resembling an undersea kite. Little skates average 16 to 20 inches long, and 8 to 16 inches wide.

Range: Outside of Narragansett Bay the little skate is found from the Gulf of St. Lawrence to North Carolina.

Behavior: The little skate is a bottom feeder and scavenger, eating primarily shellfish, crabs, amphipods, squid, worms, and small fish. Because it is covered by a series of sharp spines, most predators find it rather unappetizing. Nevertheless, it is sometimes preyed upon by large fish and marine mammals, such as sandbar sharks, monkfish, and grey seals. When it does come under attack, the little skate has a peculiar habit of curling in its tail and wings, turning itself into a spiky ball, which most predators are unable to swallow. The skate is strictly a bottom dwelling fish, and spends most of its time moving slowly along the ocean floor, resting or searching for food. It is usually found in moderately deep water over sandy bottoms, but at high tide it sometimes enters shallow water, becomes stranded, and dies as the tide recedes. It often inhabits the outer edges of eelgrass beds and is almost always found in cold, high salinity water. The little skate is found in Narragansett Bay spring through fall, and spawns in June and July. Its eggs, commonly referred to as mermaid's purses, are black and leathery, and commonly wash up on large beaches.

Relationship to People: The little skate is considered by most recreational fisherman to be an unwanted trash fish, and appears mostly as bycatch while fishing for more desirable species, like fluke and sea bass. Similarly, in southern New England, skates are generally considered pests by commercial fisherman, and are either discarded or used as bait in lobster pots. In certain parts of the world, however, skates support fairly large commercial fisheries. Most notably, they are still used in the popular English meal "fish and chips."

How to Find It: Most people would rather avoid little skates, but for those intent on finding them, doing so is pretty straightforward. They prefer moderately deep, salt water over sandy bottoms, so areas near the mouth of the Bay are ideal. Fishing with cut bait, like squid or fish, works best, but skates are by no means picky, and will bite nearly anything. Skates can also be viewed in certain locations by snorkeling or scuba diving, and are often found dead, stranded on sandy beaches at low tide.

Clearnose Skate - *Raja eglanteria*

Other Names - brier skate, summer skate

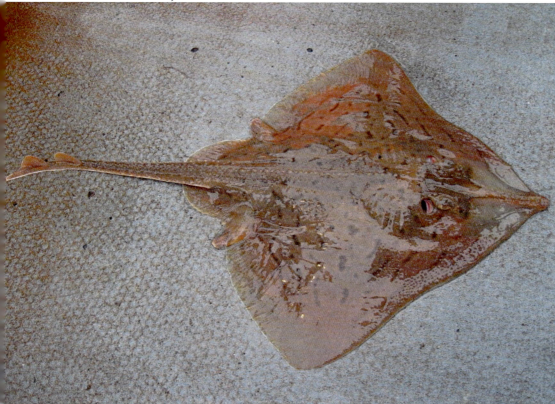

Habitat: It is found over soft bottoms in moderately deep water.

Description: On its upper side, the clearnose skate is always some shade of brown, which varies depending on its environment; underneath it is a bright white color. On top of this base color, the clearnose skate has a distinct pattern of black bars and spots. The areas of skin in front of its eyes are thin, unmarked, and translucent, (but not completely "clear" as its name would suggest). Unlike the little skate, the clearnose skate has a mostly smooth body, with the exception of a few rows of spines running along each side of the tail and one row extending along its back. Its eyes are perched on top of its head in front of two large spiracles, and it has a wide mouth with plate-like teeth below. Like other skates, it has two soft dorsal fins located far back on its tail, and instead of pectoral fins, it has two large, triangular wings. The clearnose skate has a flattened, diamond shaped body, which is more angular than that of the little skate. It averages around 2 feet long, but can grow up to 3 feet long and over 18 inches wide.

Similar Species: The barndoor skate (*Raja laevis*) is another species often found in Narragansett Bay. Like the clearnose skate, the barndoor has a pointed nose, and fairly angular body, but it lacks the black bars and translucent snout, and its underside is often pigmented. The barndoor skate is the largest skate found in the Bay, growing as large as 5 feet long, and 35 pounds. It is also found in colder waters than the clearnose skate.

Range: Outside of Narragansett Bay the clearnose skate is found from Massachusetts to Florida, and in the northern Gulf of Mexico.

Behavior: The clearnose skate is a bottom feeder and scavenger, consuming several kinds of shrimp, bivalves, squid, and small fish such as flounders, menhadens, and anchovies. Due to their large size, adult clearnose skates are only vulnerable to large inshore sharks, such as hammerheads and sand tigers. Their superb camouflage, combined with a tendency to bury themselves in the sand, keeps the skate hidden from most large predators. And if it does detect danger, the clearnose skate can burst away at high speeds with several flaps of its powerful wings. When it's not resting on the bottom, or hiding from predators, the clearnose skate is slowly scuttling along the bottom looking for food, using its pelvic fins to move in a unique "walking" motion. This species is typically found in moderately deep water over sandy bottoms not far from shore. They spawn in the summer, and after the young hatch, they have a tendency to follow large objects, such as their mothers. In Narragansett Bay, the clearnose skate is a seasonal migrant, appearing in the early summer and moving south and offshore in the winter.

Relationship to People: The clearnose skate is regarded more or less the same as the little skate by recreational and commercial anglers. For most, it is an unwanted trash fish, occasionally kept as food, (although its large size and lack of spines should make it somewhat more popular).

How to Find It: Clearnose skates are not particularly common in the Bay, although they are sometimes caught during the summer. For those determined to find them, the greatest chance of success is bottom fishing in moderately deep water over sandy bottoms, using cut fish or squid as bait.

Sharks and Rays

Smooth Dogfish -*Mustelus canis*

Other Names-dogfish, dusky smooth hound, common dogfish, smooth dog

Habitat: It is found in moderately deep water near the mouth of the Bay, in large coves and harbors, and along sandy beaches over sand and mud bottoms; it also occasionally enters large coastal rivers.

Description: Unlike most other sharks, the smooth dogfish has the ability to change its color depending on its surroundings. It varies from a purplish gray to slate brown on its back and sides, fading to a creamy white or light yellow below. Its dorsal fins and part of its caudal fin are also often edged in dark black. Its skin is rough, and covered by a series of tiny, tooth-like denticles. The smooth dogfish has pale green eyes, a downward facing mouth with blunt, crushing teeth, a sloping flat head, and a blunt snout. It has two triangular dorsal fins, free of any spines, the second of which is slightly smaller than the first. It has triangular pectoral, pelvic, and anal fins, and a typical "shark-shaped" heterocercal caudal fin. Its body shape is elongated, slender, and fusiform. It can grow to 5 feet, and over 26 pounds, but averages less than 2 feet.

Similar Species: Another species of shark sometimes found in Narragansett Bay is the spiny dogfish (***Squalus acanthius***). This species looks very similar to the smooth dogfish, but can be distinguished by the presence of two stout dorsal spines. It grows smaller than the smooth dogfish, and has similar habits, with the main difference being that it usually occurs farther from shore in deeper water.

Range: Outside of Narragansett Bay the smooth dogfish is found from the Bay of Fundy to Argentina.

Behavior: The smooth dogfish is a voracious predator, feeding on a variety of species such as clams, mantis shrimp, moon snails, squid, and fishes, particularly Atlantic menhaden and tautog. The greatest portion of its diet, however, consists of large crustaceans such as lobsters and certain crabs. Because of its size, its only real predators are larger sharks. The smooth dogfish is an active hunter, constantly prowling over the ocean bottom in search of prey. When it finds something, it seizes it in its jaws and vigorously shakes its head side-to-side before consuming it. The smooth dogfish usually hunts alone, however, if conditions are suitable, individuals sometimes hunt together in loose packs. It roams over sand and mud bottoms in harbors, bays, coastal rivers, and along large sandy beaches. Smooth dogfish are found in the Bay starting in May, remain here throughout the summer, and migrate south to deeper waters in October. They are viviparous, and females give birth to 10 to 20 live pups, from May to July.

Relationship to People: The dogfish's tendency to feed on economically valuable crustaceans, has created an unfavorable perception of this fish, particularly among crab and lobster harvesters. Commercial and recreational fishermen share this attitude, and typically view the dogfish as a nuisance that steal baits intended for other species. Thus, no significant commercial recreational fishery exists, which might not be the case if more people knew about the fish's fine table qualities, (largely a result of its primarily crustacean diet).

How to Find It: Smooth dogfish are uncommon in Narragansett Bay, however finding one isn't too difficult. Unlike spiny dogfish, which are often caught party-boat fishing for cod, smooth dogfish are found closer to shore. They're normally caught from a boat, at moderate depth, using either live or cut bait, fished at the bottom.

Miscellaneous Species

Northern Searobin -*Prionotus carolinus*

Other Names-searobin, common searobin, carolina searobin, robin, gurnard

Habitat: It is usually found in moderately deep waters over smooth, hard-packed sand bottoms, however, young fish are sometimes found close to shore in only a few feet of water, and adults sometimes enter the shallows to feed.

Description: The northern searobin's body color varies from a dusky gray to a reddish brown above, with three to five dark saddles along its back, as well as lighter web-like markings, all of which fade to a pale yellow or dirty white belly. Its dorsal, anal, and caudal fins are usually a reddish orange color, and often have light web-like markings as well. It has a distinct black spot on its spiny dorsal fin, and its pectoral fins vary from a vibrant greenish brown to dark red color. The northern searobin is easily identified by its bony head, flat shovel-like snout, and bright peacock-blue eyes. Its spiny dorsal fin is rounded, and its soft dorsal fin is elongated, mirrored below by a similar anal fin. Its caudal fin is emarginated and slightly concave, and its pectoral fins are large and fan-like, with three stiff finger-like "feelers." The searobin has an elongated, robust, tapering body. It averages less than a foot, but can grow over 17 inches long.

Similar Species: Another species, the striped searobin (*Prionotus evolans*), is also common in the Bay. The striped searobin is similar to the northern in appearance and behavior, with one key difference: a series of black lines running lengthwise along its body.

Range: Outside of Narragansett Bay the northern searobin is found from the Bay of Fundy to Central Florida.

Behavior: Despite its bizarre appearance, the northern searobin is an effective predator. It feeds on a variety of marine organisms, including squid, segmented worms, mollusks, and small fishes, but prefers crustaceans such as shrimp, crabs, and amphipods. Its main predators are larger species of fish. Unlike other bottom dwelling species, the searobin is actually quite active, and will even approach the surface at times. Most of its time, however, is spent alone, cruising across the ocean floor in search of food. It does this in a uniquely comical way, by slowly scurrying over the bottom, using its fingerlike pelvic fins to stir up the substrate and reveal any hidden prey. When it feels threatened, the searobin will rapidly bury itself, using its large pectoral fins to stir up sediment, until only its eyes and the top of its head remain visible. As its feeding habits suggest, the searobin is typically found over smooth and sandy bottoms, rather than rocky or muddy areas. The searobin moves inshore into Narragansett Bay in May, spawns from June to September, and moves offshore again in October.

Relationship to People: Because of its unwholesome appearance, the northern searobin is considered by most recreational fisherman to be an ugly bait-stealer. However, there are some devoted anglers who appreciate its fighting abilities and fine table quality, and intentionally target them for consumption. In recent years, some commercial fishermen have even begun to target them incidentally, leading to concerns about potential declines in searobin populations.

How to Find It: Northern searobins are relatively common in Narragansett Bay, and can be found using a variety of methods. They prefer moderately deep water, and are often caught while fluke fishing, using squid and other kinds of cut bait. They can also often be viewed underwater by scuba diving, and occasionally by snorkeling. Juvenile searobins are also sometimes caught seining.

Miscellaneous Species

Oyster Toadfish -*Opsanus tau*

Other Names-toadfish, dowdy

Habitat: It is usually found in shallow waters over a variety of sand, mud, and mixed bottoms. It is commonly associated with oyster reefs and man-made objects like dock pilings and piers, and is often associated with marine vegetation such as seaweed and eelgrass.

Description: The toadfish is olive brown over most of its body, fading slightly to a light tan color below. In addition, it typically has a variable pattern of darker blotches and stripes covering most of its lower body and fins. Its body is scaleless, and covered in a thick layer of slime. The most distinctive feature of the toadfish is its bizarre head, which is disproportionally large and compressed, and covered by several fleshy nobs and flaps of skin. Its mouth is large and wide, and contains a series of strong, blunt teeth. The toadfish has large, wide gill covers, with several sharp spines used for defense. It has a small spiny dorsal fin, and a larger elongated soft dorsal fin. The anal fin is similar to the second dorsal fin and the caudal and pectoral fins are rounded and fanlike. Its overall body shape is similar to that of a tadpole, with a bulky head and fat belly narrowing to a thin tail. The toadfish does not grow very large, averaging only 4 to 8 inches, but can grow as long as 15 inches.

Range: Outside of Narragansett Bay the oyster toadfish is found from Cape Cod to North Florida.

Behavior: The oyster toadfish is a greedy predator, feeding on shrimp, squid, mollusks, worms, crabs, small fish, and most notably oysters, which it can consume thanks to its strong, crushing jaws. It is in turn preyed upon by a variety of larger fish. The toadfish lives a solitary, sedentary lifestyle, spending most of its time hiding in hollows or dens, either under rocks, amongst eelgrass, or in discarded human debris, like cans or tires. It does this to both hide from potential predators, and to ambush unsuspecting prey. The toadfish can be found in a variety of shallow coastal habitats, over all kinds of ocean bottoms, but is particularly common around oyster reefs, or amongst submerged vegetation, like eelgrass beds. One unique behavior of the oyster toadfish is its ability to produce a series of loud foghorn-like vocal sounds. The male toadfish uses these sounds to attract females over long distances during the mating season. After mating, the male will guard the fertilized eggs for about a month until they hatch, and then protect the developing larvae for another few weeks until they can survive on their own. The toadfish spawns from April to October, and found in the Bay year-round.

Relationship to People: T toadfish is regarded by commercial and re reational fisherman, as a loathsome tra fish, because it greedily consumes baits tended for more prestigious game fish, a bites viciously when caught. It is, howev frequently used in different types of resear because of its low sensitivity to pollutio ability to survive out of water for long pe ods of time, and human-like eardrums. fact, two toadfish have even traveled on NASA mission into space.

How to Find It: The toadfish is not e pecially common in Narragansett Bay, bu can still be found in several places. Lar toadfish are sometimes caught while fishi in shallow rocky water for species like flu and scup, using cut fish or squid as ba Smaller toadfish can be caught by seining dragging hand nets through shallow wa with vegetation, especially in eelgrass be They are also often caught in bait traps a lobster pots set in shallow rocky water.

Miscellaneous Species

Northern Puffer -*Sphoeroides maculatus*
Other Names-puffer, blowfish, swellfish, toadfish, sea squab

Habitat: It is typically found in protected inshore waters, over sandy and muddy bottoms, and around eelgrass beds.

Description: The northern puffer's overall color varies from a greenish brown to light bronze color above, fading to a lighter pale yellow on the sides, and a creamy white belly below. On top of this base coloration there is a variable pattern of irregular black saddles and blotches along its sides. Instead of scales, the puffer is covered with a series of small prickles, which give its skin the texture of sandpaper. It has medium sized eyes and a small mouth with teeth fused into a powerful crushing beak. Another distinctive feature of the northern puffer is its crescent-shaped, slit-like gills located directly in front of its pectoral fins. It has one small soft dorsal fin located far back on its body, mirrored below by a similar anal fin. Its caudal fin is truncate and slightly rounded, and it lacks pelvic fins. Its overall body shape is rounded and boxlike, but when it is disturbed, it inflates and becomes spherical in shape. Puffers average 8 to 10 inches long, but sometimes grow up to 14 inches.

Range: Outside of Narragansett Bay the northern puffer is found from Newfoundland to North Florida.

Behavior: Juvenile puffers feed primarily on small species like copepods and larval crustaceans, while adults aggressively prey upon a wide range of invertebrates including crabs, shrimps, barnacles, sea urchins, and various kinds of mollusks. Puffers occasionally fall prey to larger species such as bluefish, summer flounder, and striped bass. They are not normally targeted, however, because when they feel threatened, they inflate themselves with water and become too large for most predators to swallow. (They can also inflate with air when held out of water). Northern puffers travel either individually or in small groups, and spend most of their time near the bottom, either lying buried in the mud or slowly milling around, looking for food. The northern puffer lives in a range of coastal habitats, in varying degrees of salinity, but is especially common over mud and sand bottoms, particularly around eelgrass beds. The northern puffer is found in Narragansett Bay from late spring through midfall, before moving offshore to deeper waters in the winter. It spawns in the Bay from June until the end of summer.

Relationship to People: The northern puffer is generally regarded by recreational anglers as an unwanted bait stealer, however, it does make fine table fare, if properly cleaned, and is not poisonous like many other species of puffers. There is also a modest commercial fishery for puffers, which have traditionally been marketed under the name "sea squab." Northern puffers are also popular in the aquarium industry, as they are fairly easy to keep, and make interesting tank inhabitants.

How to Find It: The northern puffer is more common in the Mid-Atlantic States than in RI, nevertheless it can still be found in certain places around the Bay. Larger fish are sometimes caught when bottom fishing for species like scup and fluke, but targeting them this way is usually unproductive. The most effective way to catch a northern puffer is by seining through an eelgrass bed with a sand or mud bottom. Puffers can also be caught by snorkeling or diving in shallow waters, using a slurp gun or hand net.

Miscellaneous Species

Naked Goby - *Gobiosoma bosci*

Other Names-goby, clinging goby

Habitat: It can be found in a variety of different habitats, especially over mud and shell bottoms. It is common around oyster reefs, salt marshes, and likes aquatic vegetation such as seaweed and eelgrass.

Description: The naked goby varies in color depending on its age and the environment in which it is found. Juveniles are typically a light tannish green overall, covered by a darker marbled pattern. As they grow larger, naked gobies turn purplish black in color and have a series of vertical stripes running along their body. The naked goby gets its name from its skin which is scaleless and slippery to the touch. It has a wide mouth and large eyes set on top of its partially flattened, compact head. The naked goby has a small, rounded spiny dorsal fin and an elongated soft dorsal fin, which is mirrored below by a slightly shorter anal fin. It has a wide, rounded caudal fin, large fanlike pectoral fins, and short pelvic fins which come together to form a disc-shaped suction device. Its body is elongated, stocky, vertically compressed, and somewhat tadpole-like. The naked goby is a small fish, averaging less than an inch long, but sometimes growing to two and a half inches.

Range: Outside of Narragansett Bay the naked goby can be found from Massachusetts to Florida, as well as the Gulf of Mexico.

Behavior: Because of the naked goby's small size, its diet is limited to small organisms such as worms, copepods, crustaceans, and fish fry. Gobies themselves provide prey for a wide array of species, including crabs, mantis shrimps, eels, flounders, and several other large fish species. The goby is a bottom-dwelling species, and is often found hiding amongst clumps of seaweed or inside the abandoned shells of clams and oysters. It is a fairly sluggish fish, and spends most of its time lying on the bottom, moving only in short bursts to escape predators or search for prey. Although they are not by any means schooling fish, they are not territorial either, and often occur in large numbers relatively close to one another. The naked goby can be found in nearly any relatively clean shallow coastal habitat, from salt marsh estuaries with mud bottoms, to oyster reefs, rocky bottoms with seaweed, and even eelgrass beds. It lives in Narragansett Bay year-round, lying dormant in deep water during the winter, moving inshore in early spring, and remaining there throughout the summer until late fall. Naked gobies spawn from spring until late summer, after which the males aggressively defend the fertilized eggs until th[ey] hatch.

Relationship to People: Becau[se] of its small size, the naked goby is of no [in]terest to commercial or recreational fishe[r]man. It is, however, important for scienti[sts] researching marine ecosystems, because [it] serves as a good indicator of estuarine heal[th.] Gobies are also popular with aquarists, b[e]cause they are small, easy to care for, a[nd] fairly interesting to watch.

How to Find It: The naked goby is ve[ry] common in Narragansett Bay, and can [be] caught in several different ways. Bait tra[ps] work well when placed over muddy botton[s,] but take a comparatively long time to sho[w] results. Seine nets work too, however, gobi[es] are often lost among everything else that g[ets] caught in the net. The best method, by far, [is] dragging a large hand net along a vegetat[ed] muddy bottom in shallow water. Naked g[o]bies can also be observed by snorkeling ne[ar] shore among rocks, oyster reefs, or eelgra[ss] beds. One simply has to keep their ey[es] trained on the bottom.

Miscellaneous Species

Rock Gunnel - *Pholis gunnellus*
Other Names - gunnel, butterfish, rock eel

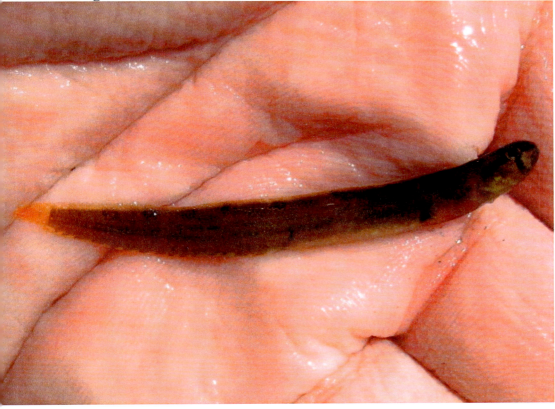

Habitat: It lives very close to shore, often right below the low tide line, and is common in rocky areas, amongst seaweed, in tide pools, and in eelgrass beds.

Description: The rock gunnel varies in color from a light yellowish green to reddish brown along its back and sides, fading to a pale yellowish belly. Along the base of the dorsal fin it has a series of dark irregular blotches, as well as a light saw-like pattern along the base of its anal fin. The rock gunnel also has a bright reddish-orange caudal fin, and a distinctive vertical black bar going through its eye to the back of its mouth. It has very small scales, and is covered in a layer of thick mucus. It has a short head with small eyes and a small mouth. It has small pectoral fins, and a small rounded caudal fin. It has one long soft dorsal fin that runs along the length of its upper body, and a similar anal fin that runs halfway along its lower body. The rock gunnel is sometimes confused with an eel, but unlike true eels, their dorsal, caudal, and anal fins are distinctly separate, and not fused together. Its body shape is extremely elongate, eel-like, and very thin. It can grow to 12 inches long, but averages just 2 to 3 inches.

Range: Outside of Narragansett Bay the rock gunnel is found from Labrador to Delaware Bay. It is also found in the eastern North Atlantic off Europe.

Behavior: The rock gunnel feeds on several kinds of marine invertebrates, including mollusks, amphipods, shrimps, and worms. It is in turn vulnerable to larger species of fish, especially the Atlantic cod. The rock gunnel is a benthic species, and is usually found lying curled up underneath rocks, in discarded shells, or amongst clumps of marine vegetation. It moves slowly by crawling like a snake along the ocean floor, unless it is startled, in which case it darts away towards cover in a short burst of speed. Rock gunnels are not territorial, and multiple fish often reside in the same small area. They can be found in a variety of near shore habitats, especially those with vegetation such as seaweed and eelgrass, however, they are usually associated with rocky shorelines. Rock gunnels are one of the few fish that remain in the intertidal zone at low tide, and are commonly found in tide pools. This is thanks to their unique ability to survive out of water for long periods of time, as long as they're protected in moist areas among seaweed or rocks. The rock gunnel is found in Narragansett Bay year round, and moves to deeper water in the winter to spawn and escape cold temperatures.

Relationship to People: Because of its small size, the rock gunnel has no value to commercial or recreational fisherman. Its only value to people is as an aquarium fish, and as a study subject in scientific research. For most people, however, a rock gunnel is merely a unique curiosity.

How to Find It: The rock gunnel is not particularly abundant in Narragansett Bay, but finding one is easy with the right techniques. They are common along the rocky coasts and in the eelgrass beds of the southern Bay, but can sometimes be found in the upper Bay as well. Rock gunnels can be caught with bait traps or by dragging a hand net along the bottom, although these methods are not very selective. Seining through eelgrass is certainly the most efficient way of catching one. They can also be found by flipping over rocks in tidepools, and by snorkeling in shallow rocky water.

Miscellaneous Species

Striped Cusk-Eel - *Ophidion marginatum*

Other Names- cusk-eel, slippery dick

Habitat: It is usually found in shallow protected waters with fine sand bottoms.

Description: The striped cusk-eel is a tannish brown color along its back and sides with a bright white belly below. In addition to this basic coloration it has a series of two or three dark stripes that run horizontally along its body. These stripes are faint in young fish, and become bolder as the fish grows older and larger. It also has dark edges on its dorsal and anal fins. The cusk-eel's head shape varies according to its sex; females have a smooth sloping head, and males have a large humplike crest. It has a fairly large inferior mouth, and large eyes common to all nocturnal fish. The striped cusk eel has medium-sized rounded pectoral fins, and two modified pelvic fins underneath its chin, often referred to as "feelers." Its dorsal, caudal, and anal fins are all fused together like those of an eel, (although like the rock gunnel, the cusk eel is not a true eel). Its body is elongated, eel-like, and thin. Cusk-eels can grow up to 10 inches long, but average 4 to 6 inches long.

Range: Outside of Narragansett Bay the striped cusk-eel is found from Cape Cod to North Florida.

Behavior: The striped cusk-eel is a bottom feeder, and consumes a variety of small invertebrates, especially the common shore shrimp. Cusk-eels are sometimes preyed upon by larger species of fish such as summer flounder and striped bass, although they have several ways of escaping predation. The cusk-eel is a completely nocturnal fish, spending all daylight hours buried in the sand with only the tip of its head poking out; it emerges only under the cover of darkness to hunt for its prey. It is also extremely wary, and will disappear tail-first, burrowing deep into the sand, at the slightest hint of danger. And even if the cusk-eel does happen to get swallowed by a predator, it has been known to use its unique burrowing ability to dig through its predator's stomach lining, into its body cavity, killing the predator in the process, (although the cusk-eel does end up dying as well). Cusk-eels are found almost exclusively in areas with fine sand bottoms, and they prefer protected areas like estuaries. This fish is found in Narragansett Bay during the summer months, and spawns from mid-June to September. During the spawning season male cusk-eels produce a loud clicking sound in an attempt to attract females.

Relationship to People: Because of their secretive behavior, cusk-eels are rarely encountered by commercial or recreational fishermen. They do, however, provide an important food source to certain commercially valuable species, especially in the southern part of their range where they are more plentiful. Cusk-eels also have an indirect significance, in that their burrowing abilities help to redistribute bottom sediments. The vocal abilities of cusk-eels are also of interest to researchers, who are still working to understand their complex calls.

How to Find It: The striped cusk-eel is very rare in Narragansett Bay, and because of its strictly nocturnal behavior, it is extremely difficult to find. The best option for someone determined to find cusk-eels is to travel south to one of the Mid-Atlantic States, and go after them at night using seine nets or bait traps, (and even this is still hit or miss). Finding one in Narragansett Bay would be a case of pure luck.

Miscellaneous Species

Barrelfish -*Hyperoglyphe perciformis*

Other Names-American barrelfish, rudderfish, polefish, logfish, black rudderfish

Habitat: It is often found amongst seaweed and other debris blown in from the open ocean. Adults are found offshore, deep in submarine canyons.

Description: As an adult, the barrelfish [is] very dark in color, ranging from greenish [gr]ay to purplish black, and fading slightly to[w]ards the belly (but usually not to a pure [w]hite like most fishes). Juveniles are much [li]ghter overall, but often have darker stripes [an]d mottling. The barrelfish has a distinc[ti]vely rounded head and blunt snout, with a [sm]all mouth and large eyes. It has one long, [co]ntinuous dorsal fin, whose spiny portion is [lo]wer than the soft portion (this disparity is [m]ore obvious in adults than juveniles). It has [a] long rectangular anal fin, a slightly forked [ca]udal fin, and relatively large, rounded pel[vi]c fins. Its overall body shape is stout, some[w]hat elongate, and similar to that of a young [t]utog. It is a fairly large fish, growing up to [3]5 inches, and 25 pounds, although those [fo]und in the Bay are juveniles, and only grow [to] a few inches long.

Range: Outside of Narragansett Bay the [ba]rrelfish is found from Nova Scotia to Flori[d]a. It is also found in the eastern Gulf of [M]exico, and in the northeastern Atlantic [fr]om the British Isles to Portugal.

Behavior: The barrelfish feeds on a variety of pelagic organisms such as squid, crustaceans, mollusks, small fish, salps, hydroids, and ctenophores. It is in turn vulnerable to terns and other diving birds, as well as large fish like bluefish and tuna. Barrelfish are an archetypical pelagic species, especially as juveniles. Young fish are typically found far out at sea, drifting just below the surface, amongst floating mats of seaweed and debris such as wreckage, planks, or barrels (which is where they get their name). Oftentimes during the summer, this floating debris, sheltering large schools of juvenile barrelfish, is blown into coastal waters, such as those of Narragansett Bay. Here, the juveniles develop for several weeks, hiding in the shallows amongst debris and seaweed, until they are large enough to move to their proper home. As adults, barrelfish live offshore in submarine canyons, in water often several hundreds of feet deep. Much is still unknown about the lifestyles of adult barrelfish, due in part to the great depths at which they reside, but it is believed that they travel in schools above the bottom.

Relationship to People: Until recently, barrelfish were relatively unknown to commercial and recreational fisherman, simply because adults were seldom encountered. But with advances in technology, it has now become easier to fish at the great depths this species calls home. Over the past few years, recreational fishermen have also discovered that not only does the barrelfish grow large and put up a decent fight, it also makes fine table fare. A small commercial fishery for this species has even sprouted up off the southeastern United States. Unfortunately, only juveniles are found in the Bay, and these are merely curiosities.

How to Find It: The barrelfish is rare in Narragansett Bay, yet a few juveniles are usually found each summer. The best places to look are areas where debris naturally washes up, particularly coves near the mouth of the Bay. They are typically found hiding amongst seaweed or underneath floating objects, and can be caught by seining, or with the quick swipe of a hand net.

Miscellaneous Species

Atlantic Needlefish -*Strongylura marina*

Other Names-needlefish, silver gar, garfish, billfish, sea pike, agujon

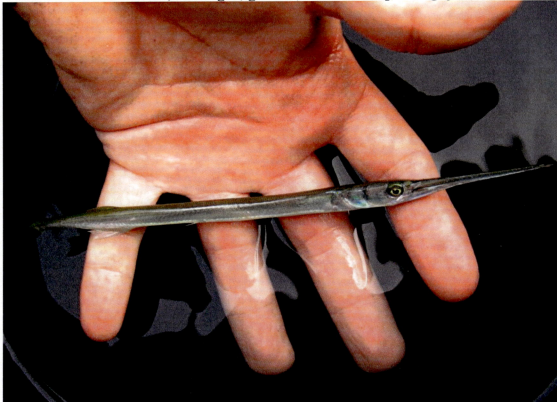

Habitat: It lives in shallow coastal waters, particularly in sheltered areas such as harbors, estuaries, salt marsh coves, eelgrass beds, and even well into coastal streams.

Description: The Atlantic needlefish is a pale green color above, fading to a shiny silver on its sides, and a white belly below. It has a faint iridescent stripe running along the middle of its body, and its fins are more or less transparent. It has small scales, and is very smooth to the touch. The needlefish has a distinctly elongated bony head, fairly large eyes, and a disproportionately long set of jaws, filled with a series of tiny needlelike teeth. It has one slightly concave, semi-triangular, soft dorsal fin, located far back on its body. Underneath and slightly forward of the dorsal fin, the needlefish has a similarly shaped anal fin. It has a slightly forked caudal fin, small rounded pectoral fins, and small pelvic fins located in the middle of its body. It has a thick, slender, somewhat serpentine body shape. The needlefish averages around a foot, but is known to grow up to 4 feet long.

Range: Outside of Narragansett Bay the Atlantic needlefish ranges from Maine to Florida, as well as the Gulf of Mexico, and the Caribbean coasts of Central and South America, to Brazil.

Behavior: Atlantic needlefish share many similar behaviors with young "snapper" bluefish. They initially feed on copepods, mysids, and small shrimp, but as they grow larger their diet shifts towards small schooling fish, such as silversides, anchovies, and young menhaden. The needlefish's predators include sea birds, dolphins, and larger species of fish, such as bluefish and striped bass. The needlefish is fairly active both day and night, and hunts in pairs or small groups by slowly prowling a few inches below the water's surface. Once it encounters a school of baitfish, it rushes forward in a burst of speed, and seizes any unlucky fish it can in its spiky jaws. When it is being pursued by predators, the Atlantic needlefish has a unique and effective habit of jumping clear out of the water to evade capture. It is found in a variety of protected coastal habitats, from salt marsh coves, to sheltered eelgrass beds, and even the brackish portions of tidal rivers. Since Narragansett Bay is in the northern part of its range, the needlefish is only present here during summer and early fall, before moving south in mid-October.

Relationship to People: Because of its small size and strictly coastal habit the Atlantic needlefish is seldom encountered by commercial fishermen, and is of great economic value. Where they are common, needlefish are regarded by recreation fishermen as nuisances, however, here in t Bay they are rare enough that they wou likely be viewed more as curiosities. T needlefish's unique anguilliform swimmi motion also make it an interesting subject scientists studying fish locomotion.

How to Find It: The Atlantic needl fish is fairly uncommon in Narragansett B however, there are certain places where person might find one. They are almost ways found in fairly shallow protected w ters, particularly in areas with a high conce tration of baitfish. Harbors, estuaries, s marsh coves, eelgrass beds, and river mout are the best places to search for needlefis They can be caught by fishing with a snapp bluefish rig, or with small strips of cut-ba However, the most efficient way to cat them is with a seine net.

Sculpins

Grubby Sculpin - *Myoxocephalus aenaeus*

Other Names - grubby, little sculpin, brassy sculpin, sculpin

Habitat: It is found in shallow coastal waters over a variety of bottoms, especially among rocks, seaweed, and eelgrass beds. It is also common in tidepools.

Description: Like most bottom-dwelling species, the grubby sculpin has a range of color variations that depend on the habitat in which it is found. They can be anything from a reddish orange to a grayish green color, although most are some shade of brown. Fortunately, all grubby sculpins have one large dark saddle below the first dorsal fin, and two smaller saddles below the second dorsal fin, all of which fade into a mottled region and eventually a white belly. Its head is dark and mottled, and its fins are a light reddish brown color with a variety of darker markings. It has a large bulky head with big eyes, a large inferior mouth, and several short spines. The grubby has a somewhat rounded spiny dorsal fin and a slightly elongated soft dorsal fin. It has a fairly small rounded caudal fin and very large fanlike pectoral fins. Its overall body shape is very short and stocky, like that of a tadpole. It does not grow very large and is usually only a few inches long, but can reach up to 5 inches.

Range: Outside of Narragansett Bay the grubby sculpin is found from the Gulf of St. Lawrence to New Jersey.

Behavior: Despite its small size the grubby sculpin is an opportunistic predator and scavenger. It feeds primarily on crustaceans such as amphipods, crabs, and shrimp, but will eat almost anything, including marine worms, snails, and a host of small fish. The grubby sculpin is a passive hunter, lying in wait along the ocean floor, using its superb camouflage to conceal itself from unsuspecting prey. This camouflage is also the sculpin's greatest defense against predators such as flounders, striped bass, diving birds, and large crustaceans. The grubby sculpin is strictly a bottom dwelling fish, and spends most of its time inactive, moving only in occasional bursts to avoid predators or pursue prey. They can be found in several coastal habitats, particularly amongst rocks, seaweed, and eelgrass, and are one of the few fish that are commonly found in tide pools. Like most sculpins, the grubby can tolerate extremely cold temperatures, and spawns in the middle of winter. It is much more tolerant of warmer temperatures, however, than other sculpin species, and is readily found throughout the Bay year-round.

Relationship to People: Like other members of the sculpin family, the grubby sculpin has no commercial or recreational value to most fisherman. Fortunately it is small enough that most fishermen simply do not encounter it, although occasionally large ones are caught on very light tackle. This lack of attention means that grubby sculpin populations are fairly healthy.

How to Find It: The grubby sculpin is common in Narragansett Bay, and can be found in several different ways. One unique way of observing the grubby in its natural habitat is by "tide-pooling." This involves going to a rocky area where large pools are left by the outgoing tide, and waiting by the side of one of these pools, looking for movement which typically signifies a fish. Bait traps and seine nets are also effective methods for catching sculpins. The easiest way to find one, however, is by snorkeling. Any shallow, clear water with rocks and seaweed is bound to be home to a few grubby sculpins. One simply has to move slowly and look carefully to find them.

Sculpins
Longhorn Sculpin -*Myoxocephalus octodecemspinosus*

Other Names-gray sculpin, common sculpin, spined sculpin, hacklehead, toadfish

Habitat: It is found in cold water over a variety of bottom types. In southern New England they are found offshore in the summer, and move inshore in the winter.

Description: Like the grubby, the longhorn sculpin has a wide range of color variations, and can appear in shades of red, orange, green, and brown, all fading to a white belly. Most of the time, the longhorn sculpin has four irregular crossbars running along its body, but these are often distorted and difficult to notice. Its fins vary in color with the rest of its body, and are marked with an assortment of blotches, spots, and striations. The longhorn sculpin has a large, blunt, box-like head with large eyes and a large mouth. Its most distinguishing feature is its extremely long preopercular spine, which is longer than that of any other north Atlantic sculpin. Its spiny dorsal fin is high and rounded, and its soft dorsal fin is curved and somewhat elongate, as is its anal fin. It has a rounded caudal fin and large fan-like pectoral fins. Its body shape is elongate, slender, slightly tapering, and somewhat tadpole-like. It is larger than the grubby, growing up to 18 inches, and averaging about a foot.

Similar Species: The shorthorn sculpin (*Myoxocephalus scorpius*) is very similar in appearance and behavior to the longhorn sculpin. The primary difference between the two is, as their names suggests, the length of their preopercular spines, (it is shorter in the shorthorn sculpin). The shorthorn can also grow much larger than the longhorn, up to 3 feet.

Range: Outside of Narragansett Bay the longhorn sculpin is found from Newfoundland and the Gulf of St. Lawrence to Virginia.

Behavior: The longhorn sculpin is a voracious omnivore and scavenger, feeding on a wide range of crabs, worms, shrimp, mussels, squid, and small fish. In fact, the longhorn sculpin is often found in harbors with heavy commercial fishing traffic, simply because of the ready access to discarded fish remains. Like the grubby, the longhorn is a fairly sluggish fish that spends most of its time either resting or slowly milling about on the ocean floor in search of food. It is found over a variety of bottom types, in a wide range of depths, although it is decidedly a cold-water fish. So in southern New England, longhorn sculpins tend to remain offshore in deep, cool waters during the summer, and when winter arrives, they move en masse towards the coast. But in t[he] northern parts of their range, longhorn sc[ul]pins are found inshore during the summ[er] and move offshore in the winter to avo[id] extremely cold temperatures. They spa[wn] from November to February, with peak a[c]tivity occurring in the dead of winter.

Relationship to People: T[he] longhorn sculpin, like the rest of its fami[ly] is unpopular amongst commercial and re[c]reational fishermen. Its unappealing appea[r]ance, small size, weak game qualities, a[nd] bait-stealing tendencies put it at the botto[m] of most anglers' target list. Its only notab[le] use is as bait in lobster pots.

How to Find It: Longhorn sculpi[ns] are not particularly common in the Bay, b[ut] they can be found if one is so inclined. Th[ey] require cold water, and are often caug[ht] deep-sea-fishing on party or charter boa[ts,] especially in the fall. They can be caug[ht] near shore during the winter, although [an] easier (and warmer) method for someo[ne] determined to see one, would be to trav[el] north to Maine or Massachusetts, a[nd] search there during the summer.

Pipefish and Seahorses
Northern Pipefish -*Sygnathus fuscus*
Other Names-pipefish, common pipefish

Habitat: It is typically associated with aquatic vegetation such as seaweed and eelgrass beds. It prefers protected areas such as bays, harbors, rocky coves and salt marsh ponds, and sometimes enters brackish water.

Description: The northern pipefish's coloration varies widely depending on its environment, with individuals appearing anywhere from dark dusky brown to light olive green above, and light white to greenish yellow below. Certain fish will also have a light vertical banding pattern on top of this base coloring. Rather than scales, the pipefish has smooth skin covering a series of rigid, bony plates. It has a small, elongated head, large gill plates, and medium sized eyes. Its snout is long and tube-like, with a very small toothless mouth at the tip. It has one rectangular soft dorsal fin located in the middle of its body, small rounded pectoral fins, and a small, fanlike caudal fin. It has a tiny rounded anal fin, and it lacks pelvic fins. The pipefish has an extremely elongated and slender body, with a relatively thick midsection before the dorsal fin, and a thin tail afterwards. It averages 3 to 7 inches long, but can grow up to 12 inches.

Range: Outside of Narragansett Bay the northern pipefish can be found from the Gulf of St. Lawrence to North Florida. It is also found in the northern Gulf of Mexico.

Behavior: Because of the small size of its mouth, the diet of the northern pipefish is limited to tiny prey items such as copepods, brine shrimp, small marine worms, and other kinds of zooplankton. It is not commonly eaten by other fish, in part because it is very bony and not particularly appetizing, but also because of its superior abilities to escape detection. The northern pipefish's long, greenish-brown body looks very similar to many types of seaweed and eelgrass. The pipefish uses this resemblance to its advantage by lying in and amongst clumps of seaweed when trying to hide from predators. In fact, it is a fairly sedentary species, and spends most of its time either lying motionless on the bottom or slowly drifting with the current. Like many species, however, it is capable of quick bursts of speed when it is startled and needs to escape from potential danger. The northern pipefish can be found anywhere with an abundance of aquatic vegetation, including bays, harbors, salt ponds, rocky coves and a variety of other coastal habitats, although they are most common in eelgrass beds. The pipefish arrives in Narragansett Bay in the spring, spawns throughout the summer until August, and migrates offshore to deeper water in the winter.

Relationship to People: Because of its relatively small size, and bony body, the pipefish is of no interest to commercial or recreational fisherman. Also, because it is not typical prey for most fish species, it is almost never used as bait. The pipefish's main importance to humans is in the aquarium trade, as they are fairly easy to care for and interesting to watch.

How to Find It: The northern pipefish is common in Narragansett Bay, and very easy to find. From May until October, any shallow water with seaweed is likely to have them, especially eelgrass beds. As one would expect, pipefish cannot be caught on rod and reel; fortunately, other methods work just fine. Bait traps can be effective, but nets are faster and more efficient, especially seine nets. In fact, when seining in certain areas, one can catch more than 75 pipefish per seine. Pipefish can also be observed by snorkeling through eelgrass beds or other shallow vegetated environments.

Lined Seahorse - *Hippocampus erectus*

Pipefish and Seahorses

Other Names-seahorse, northern seahorse, common seahorse, spotted seahorse

Habitat: It is found almost exclusively in healthy eelgrass beds.

Description: The lined seahorse is easily the most unmistakable fish in Narragansett Bay. Like other species that rely on camouflage for protection, the seahorse can appear in many different colors. It can be ashy gray, dusky brown, even a bright greenish-yellow, and is often covered by spots, blotches, and other variable markings. Its body is constructed of bony plates, and it has smooth skin with several fleshy protuberances and filaments. It has a distinctive "horse-shaped" head, with a tube-like snout, medium-sized eyes, and large gill plates. It has a moderate-sized soft dorsal fin located in the middle of its body, medium-sized pectoral fins located right behind the gill plates, and a miniscule anal fin located below its belly. The body shape of the lined seahorse is unlike any other fish in the Bay, and is somewhat reminiscent of the "knight" piece from a chess set, with a wide rounded belly, tapering to a long flexible tail. The seahorse averages between 3 and 4 inches, but sometimes reaches over 7 inches long.

Range: Outside of Narragansett Bay the lined seahorse is found from Nova Scotia to Argentina, including the Gulf of Mexico and the Caribbean Sea.

Behavior: Like the pipefish, the seahorse's diet is limited by its small tube-like snout, to tiny marine invertebrates such as copepods, amphipods, mysid shrimps, small worms, and other types of zooplankton. The lined seahorse is potentially vulnerable to any species of fish with a mouth large enough to swallow it, although fortunately most predators can never find it in the first place. In fact, nearly everything about the seahorse is catered towards avoiding detection. Its body is perfectly camouflaged to blend in with aquatic vegetation, and it spends the majority of its time clinging to seaweed with its prehensile tail, looking like just another blade of eelgrass. When it does move, it does so very slowly, swimming in an upright position with its tail extended, so that it appears to be drifting freely with the current. The lined seahorse is almost always found in large, healthy eelgrass beds. It is strictly solitary, except during the breeding season when males and females join together in monogamous pairs. After engaging in elaborate courtship rituals prior to mating, the male seahorse gives birth to live young, in a unique role reversal. The seahorse found in the Bay from spring through fa spawns in the summer, and moves offsho in the winter.

Relationship to People: Like t pipefish, the seahorse has no value to co mercial or recreational fisherman in Nar gansett Bay. In other parts of the world, ho ever, they are collected in large numbers f use in traditional medicine. Here in the Ba they are one of the top prizes for amateur a uarists, as they are beautiful, hard to fin and fairly easy to care for.

How to Find It: Although finding lin seahorses in Narragansett Bay is relative uncommon, targeting them is quite straig forward. They live almost exclusively in ee grass beds, so one need not look elsewhe Large beds near the mouth of the Bay are t most productive, but there is never a guara tee of success. Because they move slowl they can be caught while snorkeling, a hough they are usually tough to spot, so sei ing is the preferred method.

Sticklebacks
Fourspine Stickleback - *Apeltes quadracus*

Other Names - stickleback, pinfish, mud perch, bloody stickleback

Habitat: It is typically found near shore in areas with plenty of aquatic vegetation, particularly eelgrass beds, salt marshes, and tidal creeks. It also enters brackish water, and can even be found in freshwater streams and ponds.

Description: The fourspine stickleback an olive green to dark brown color above, ding to a silvery white below. Much of its per body is also covered by a highly variable dark mottling. Its fins are reddish own, and during the breading season ales develop a bright scarlet red color on eir pelvic fins. It's easily distinguished om the threespine stickleback by its nooth and scaleless skin. It has relatively rge eyes, and a relatively small mouth. he fourspine stickleback derives its name om the four (sometimes five) spines located along its back. The first three (or four) re separate, and the last one is attached to s soft dorsal fin, which is mirrored below y a slightly smaller anal fin. The fourspine ickleback has a thin caudal peduncle, with small rounded caudal fin, and its pelvic ns are stout and spiny. It has a fusiform, pering body, with two bony ridges along s abdomen which give it a somewhat triangular cross-section. It is a small fish, averaging 1½ to 2½ inches.

Range: Outside of Narragansett Bay the urspine stickleback is found from the Gulf f St. Lawrence to North Carolina, and has been introduced into much of the eastern United States, and southern Canada.

Behavior: As its small size suggests, the fourspine stickleback is rather low on the Bay's food chain. It feeds primarily on copepods and other small marine invertebrates, and is vulnerable to predation by mantis shrimp, crabs, wading birds, and many species of fish such as sculpins, flounders, and bluefish. Its main means of defense are the sharp spines along its back and its tendency to live near shore in areas with a lot of aquatic vegetation, (ideal hiding places from predators). As such, it is typically found in salt marshes and eelgrass beds, although anywhere with an abundance of seaweed is likely to have a few resident sticklebacks. They also travel well into freshwater, and are common in many coastal streams. The fourspine stickleback is a predominantly solitary species, although it is often found in close proximity to other small fish. During the late spring and early summer months, however, male sticklebacks become quite territorial, as their thoughts turn to breeding. After establishing his territory, the male constructs a cone-shaped nest, in which a successfully courted female can deposit her eggs. The male then guards the nest until the eggs hatch and protects the hatchlings until they can survive on their own.

Relationship to People: The fourspine stickleback is far too small to have any commercial or recreational value as a food fish. Conceivably, it could be used as bait for larger game fish, although species like killifish and silversides are a more readily-available option. Thus, their only significant use is as subjects in scientific experiments, or as an occasional aquarium fish.

How to Find It: The fourspine stickleback is fairly easy to find in Narragansett Bay. The best places to look are shallow weedy areas like marshes, salt ponds, eelgrass beds, and even the edges of harbors. It can be caught in bait traps, although the most efficient way to catch one is using nets. Seine nets work well, although a medium-sized hand net is the simplest method. It can also be seen snorkeling, provided one is able to spot it amongst all the vegetation.

Sticklebacks
Threespine Stickleback -*Gasterosteus aculeatus*

Other Names-European stickleback, stickleback, thorn fish, thornback

Habitat: It is found near shore, in areas with abundant aquatic vegetation like salt marshes, and especially eelgrass. It is equally comfortable in salt and freshwater, and is sometimes found far from land in floating clumps of seaweed.

Description: The threespine stickleback varies in color from a light olive brown to a grayish green above and a metallic silver to brassy gold below. In addition, it sometimes has darker spots, mottling, or even faint vertical stripes. During the breeding season, adult fish, especially males, develop a bright red coloration along their heads and bellies. The threespine stickleback is covered along its sides by a series of thin, bony plates, and it has a distinct circular plate between its gills and pectoral fins. It has a large head with large eyes and a small slightly upturned mouth. As its name suggests, the threespine stickleback has three dorsal spines, two of which are separate from the soft dorsal fin, and one of which is attached. This stickleback has a slightly emarginate caudal fin, a triangular anal fin, stout pelvic fins, and rounded pectoral fins. Its body shape is thinner and more elongate than the fourspine stickleback. The threespine stickleback grows to a maximum of 4 inches but is usually between 1½ and 2 inches long.

Similar Species: The ninespine stickleback (***Pungitius pungitius***) is also often found in Narragansett Bay. This species prefers brackish water more than saltwater, and is most common in coastal rivers. The ninespine stickleback is similar to the threespine in many respects, although its mouth is more upturned and it lacks the defined circular plate between the gills and pectoral fins. The most obvious difference between the two is that the ninespine stickleback has 7 to 12 dorsal spines.

Range: Outside of Narragansett Bay the threespine stickleback is found in most subarctic waters from North America to Eurasia.

Behavior: Despite its small size, the threespine stickleback is a surprisingly aggressive predator. This fish greedily feeds on anything it can, including fish fry, copepods, isopods, young squid, small invertebrates, and algae. Like the fourspine stickleback, the threespine stickleback is vulnerable to a host of marine predators, and uses its spines as its main defense. The threespine stickleback is found in more or less the same environment as the fourspine stickleback, although it seems to be more common in eelgrass beds. It is a solitary fish, and is often aggressive towards other species in its territory, especially during mating season. However, the threespine stickleback is one of the most variable fish species ever studied. Around the world populations display completely different behaviors as they adapt to the local environmental conditions. So although in New England, threespine sticklebacks are quite aggressive, across the ocean in the United Kingdom, they tend to be more docile.

Relationship to People: In New England, the threespine stickleback has no commercial value, although in parts of Northern Europe they are common enough to be boiled down into fish oil. Their greatest value is in scientific research, where their highly variable behaviors offer an interesting insight into the processes of evolution.

How to Find It: The threespine stickleback, like the fourspine, is rather easy to find. They are found in many of the same areas, although the best spots for threespine sticklebacks are eelgrass beds. The best way to catch them is using a large seine net, although simple hand nets also work.

Killifish

Striped Killifish -*Fundulus majalus*
Other Names-striped killy, killifish, striped mummichog

Habitat: It likes salt marshes, eelgrass beds, protected harbors, sandy shorelines, areas with aquatic vegetation, and nearly any calm waters within about fifty feet of shore.

Description: The striped killifish is sexually dimorphic, meaning that its coloration is determined by its gender. Both males and females are a light olive green above fading to pale white below. The difference comes in the pattern of black bars along their body. Males have 15 to 20 vertical black bars running along the side of their body (the individual pictured above is a male), while females have 2 or 3 black stripes running horizontally. The striped killifish's fins are usually a light brown color. In the breeding season, its back turns dark black, its sides turn orange and its fins turn a brilliant yellow color. It has a small, upward-facing blunt mouth, and a sloping head with a long nose. It has one small soft dorsal fin located far back on its body, a rounded caudal fin, and large fanlike pectoral fins. Its body shape is semi-elongate, rounded and stocky. Striped killifish can grow up to 7 inches, but are usually around 1-3 inches.

Similar Species: Another species of killifish abundant in Narragansett Bay is the common mummichog (*Fundulus heteroclitus*). The mummichog is nearly identical to the striped killifish in terms of behavior, and varies only in appearance. It lacks the killifish's black stripes, instead showing white vertical bars, over an olive green background.

Range: Outside of Narragansett Bay the striped killifish ranges from New Hampshire to North Florida. It is also found in the Gulf of Mexico.

Behavior: The striped killifish preys upon a wide variety of mollusks, crustaceans, insects, insect larvae, and fish fry. Like other species of killifish, it schools with members of its own species, as well as other baitfish, for protection against a wide range of predators, including larger fish, blue crabs, and wading birds. The striped killifish is fairly ubiquitous throughout the Bay, and can be encountered in nearly any protected area close to shore. It is often seen schooling within inches of a sandy shoreline, darting in between each breaking wave. They can tolerate highly variable levels of oxygen and salinity, and when the tide recedes they can survive in stagnant pools that would quickly kill most other fish species. And if one of these pools dries up, this fish can flop head-over-tail across land until it reaches a permanent supply of water. Striped killifish stay in Narragansett Bay year round, and are most common early spring through late fall; they typically spend their winters lying buried in the mud.

Relationship to People: Because of their small size, striped killifish provide no commercial or recreational fishery, although theoretically large ones could be caught on very light tackle. The most common anthropogenic use for striped killifish is as bait, since they are easy to catch, effective for a variety of game species, and their population remains healthy.

How to Find It: The striped killifish is certainly one of the easiest fish to catch in Narragansett Bay. They can be caught in practically any shallow coastal area, (sandy shorelines are especially productive), with any type of net. However, the simplest way to catch one is with a bait trap. Striped killifish can also be observed from land, schooling in the shallow water close to shore, or underwater while snorkeling.

Killifish

Rainwater Killifish - *Lucania parva*

Other Names- killifish

Habitat: It is found primarily in large salt marsh coves among aquatic vegetation. It tolerates a wide range of salinities, from pure saltwater environments, to brackish estuaries, and even well into freshwater rivers.

Description: The rainwater killifish is a plain olive to light brown color, accentuated with light purple hues, and a creamy white belly. Near its base, its dorsal fin is sometimes edged in black, and its scales are outlined in dusky brown, creating a hexagonal cross-hatch pattern. Its fins are typically a light dusky orange color, which becomes more vibrant during the breeding season. Its nose is more rounded than other killifish; it has fairly large eyes, and a small, flat, upturned mouth. The rainwater killifish has one soft dorsal fin located near the middle of its body. Its anal fin is slightly smaller and positioned slightly farther back, and its pectoral fins are small and rounded. Like other killifish, its caudal fin is wide and rounded. Its overall body shape is somewhat elongate, but deeper than the other killifish, with the exception of the sheepshead minnow. Its back is slightly arched, and its body is fairly stocky. The rainwater killifish is smaller than most other killifish, reaching a maximum of only two inches long.

Range: Outside of Narragansett Bay the rainwater killifish can be found from Massachusetts to the northern Yucatan peninsula. It exists inland in the freshwater rivers of Florida and Texas, and has been introduced to freshwater environments in many Western states.

Behavior: Limited by its size, the rainwater killifish feeds mainly on larval crustaceans, copepods, marine worms, small mollusks, and insects, particularly mosquito pupae and larvae. They are preyed upon by a wide range of predators such as crabs, larger species of fish, and wading birds, such as herons and egrets. They would probably more vulnerable, were it not for their schooling habits and tendency to live in shallow water, with many hiding spots. Compared to most other fish species the rainwater killifish is surprisingly social. They do not school together closely, rather they roam around in loose bands, playfully chasing each other and quarreling over bits of food. Rainwater killifish will also work together to help rid each other of external parasites. To signal that it would like to be cleaned, an individual simply needs to swim vertically, nose pointed-up, and wait for another rainwater killifish to respond. This species is typically encountered in the shallow, weedy portions of salt marshes, usually in still water, and c tolerate a wide range of salinities. The ra water killifish is found in Narragansett B year round, and like other killifish, they a most common spring through fall, and spe their winters lying dormant in the mud.

Relationship to People: Than to its especially small size, the rainwater k lifish supports no commercial fishery, and only use in recreational fishing as bait, (ho ever its size and relative scarcity, make oth species preferable). It's most popular use in marine aquariums, as it is easy to care fo and its social habits make it particularly i teresting to watch.

How to Find It: The rainwater killifi is less common in the Bay than other speci of killifish, however, they are not impossib to find. Large salt marsh coves and sa ponds with abundant aquatic vegetation a the best places to look for them. They can caught with traps, and hand nets, howev the best method is certainly a large seine n

Killifish
Sheepshead Minnow - *Cyprinodon variegatus*

Other Names - variegated minnow, broad killifish

Habitat: It is usually found near shore in shallow protected areas, such as harbors, salt ponds, and salt marsh coves.

Description: The sheepshead minnow is grayish green to iridescent greenish blue above, fading to a pale white belly below. On its sides, the sheepshead minnow has a series of irregular vertical bars that range from a grayish black to a light brown color. In the breeding season, these colors become greatly exaggerated; males develop a brilliant blue nape, bright orange cheeks and belly, and lose their dark markings. The overall color of its fins are dusky brown, its caudal fin is bordered in black, and its dorsal fin has a black dot on the base of the first ray. The sheepshead minnow has a flat head, upturned nose and sharp tricuspid teeth. Like other species of killifish the sheepshead minnow has one soft dorsal fin located far back on its body, and a small rounded anal fin located below. Its caudal fin is truncate, its pelvic fins are small, and its pectoral fins are large and rounded. The overall body shape of the sheepshead minnow is deeper, shorter, and stockier than that of any other Narragansett Bay killifish, and its back is highly arched. The sheepshead minnow is a very small fish, growing to a maximum of 1½ inches long.

Range: Outside of Narragansett Bay the sheepshead minnow is found from Massachusetts to northern Mexico. They are also found on the Gulf coast and in certain inland waters in the southern United States.

Behavior: The sheepshead minnow, despite its small size, is a voracious predator. It is omnivorous, and feeds on a range of aquatic plants, algae, detritus, insect larvae, other invertebrates, and smaller fish. It is in turn preyed upon by larger fish, crabs, wading birds, and a variety of other aquatic predators. Like other species of baitfish, the sheepshead minnow often travels in loose schools with members of its own and other species. However, it is an aggressive fish, and will sometimes attack and injure larger fish, using its sharp teeth to slash its victims. Males become particularly aggressive during the mating season, and will often fight each other over territory and females. Sheepshead minnows live very close to shore in protected areas like salt marshes, salt ponds, and harbors. They can tolerate wide changes in salinity, temperature, and oxygen levels, and are often found stranded in tide-pools at low tide. These fish are found in Narragansett Bay year round, but during the winter, like other killifish, they lay dormant, buried deep in the mud.

Relationship to People: Unsurprisingly, there is no commercial or recreational fishery for the sheepshead minnow due to its small size. Its main use is as bait for recreational anglers targeting larger game species. Sheepshead minnows could easily survive in an amateur's aquarium, thanks to their tolerance of a wide range of temperature, salinity, and oxygen levels, but their aggressive nature makes keeping them with other fish problematic.

How to Find It: The sheepshead minnow is harder to find than the common mummichog or striped killifish. While one could expect to find these fish almost anywhere, sheepshead minnows require more searching. They like the edges of salt marsh coves and salt ponds, but are not found everywhere. Once they are found, however, they can be easily caught with bait traps, hand nets, or seine nets.

Alewife - *Alosa pseudoharengus*

Other Names - river herring, sawbelly, gaspereau, big-eye, glut herring, bucky

Habitat: It does not have any particular habitat preference, (except for clean over polluted waters). It is found in open water and near shore, in rocky coves, harbors, protected estuaries, salt marshes, and river mouths, especially during the breeding season.

Description: The alewife has a bluish green back, bright silvery sides, a white belly, and yellowish-brown fins outlined in black. It has very few other markings on its body, other than a small black spot sometimes present just behind its gill flap. In larger fish, the sides may appear iridescent, giving off hues of green and purple, however, these colors begin to disappear soon after capture, as the stressed fish's large, rough scales are easily brushed off. The most distinctive features of the alewife are its large eyes, relatively small head, and toothless mouth. (All of which help distinguish it from the similar-looking Atlantic menhaden). Its caudal fin is deeply forked, it has one soft dorsal fin located in the middle of its body, and a small tapering anal fin. Its overall body shape is elongate, oblong, and horizontally compressed. Alewives can grow up to 16 inches long, but are usually much smaller.

Similar Species: Another species, the blueback herring (*Alosa aestivalis*), is so similar to the alewife that the only major distinction between the two, is that blueback herring are dark blue on their backs while alewives are greenish in color. These similar appearances, combined with shared behaviors, have inspired many people to lump the two together under the single colloquial name: "river herring."

Range: Outside of Narragansett Bay the alewife can be found from Newfoundland to South Carolina. Along much of its range it is also found in inland freshwater environments.

Behavior: The alewife is mainly planktivorous, and feeds by using a series of gill rakers to filter out microorganisms from the surrounding water. They are in turn an important prey item for several species of fish, like bluefish and striped bass, as well as coastal birds, such as terns and gulls. Their main form of protection against predators, is congregating in large, tightly organized schools of similarly-sized fish. While in these schools, alewives often feed in unison, and can be seen with their mouths gaping, cruising just below the surface. They are occasionally found schooling in the company of other species as well, particularly menhaden and silversides. Alewives can be found in nearly any habitat provided the water is relatively clean, however, they prefer p[ro]tected areas like salt marshes, eelgrass be[ds] and river mouths. Alewives are well kno[wn] for their anadromous spawning habits; [in] early spring, adults ascend their natal riv[ers] en masse to deposit their eggs, before retu[rn]ing to the Bay by early summer.

Relationship to People: At o[ne] time alewives (and blueback herring), su[p]ported huge commercial and recreatio[nal] fisheries, and were caught in huge numbe[rs] during their spawning runs, for use as fo[od] and bait. Over the years, however, increas[ed] fishing pressure, along with pollution and t[he] construction of dams has led to a 95% [de]cline in their population. As a result str[ict] regulations were created, and today harve[st] or possession of river herring is illegal.

How to Find It: Because harvesti[ng] alewives is illegal, it is not recommend[ed] that one intentionally target them. Howeve[r,] they are not particularly uncommon, and a[re] sometimes caught while seining, mixed [in] amongst other species of baitfish. One c[an] also sometimes view schooling alewives [from] land, from docks or bridges.

Herrings
Atlantic Menhaden -*Brevoortia tyrannus*
Other Names-menhaden, pogy, bunker, mossbunker, fatback

Habitat: It can be found nearly anywhere, in rocky coves, amongst eelgrass beds, and along sandy beaches; larger fish are usually found in open water.

Description: The Atlantic menhaden looks very similar to the alewife in physical morphology and coloration, with a few key differences. It has an overall olive green to grayish blue coloring above, silvery sides with hues of iridescent purples and pinks, and a bright white belly. It has a distinctive black shoulder spot located directly behind its gill flap, and often times a series of smaller black spots on its sides. Its fins are typically yellowish bronze in color. The main feature used to distinguish between menhaden and alewives is its proportionally large head, which takes up one-third of its total body length. The menhaden has one soft dorsal fin located in the middle of its body, a tapering anal fin, and a deeply forked caudal fin. The menhaden has an oval body shape which is deeper than the alewife, but equally compressed. It grows as large as 18 inches long, but averages 2-4 inches.

Range: Outside of Narragansett Bay the menhaden is found from New Brunswick to South Florida.

Behavior: The menhaden, like the alewife, feeds by opening its mouth wide and allowing water to pass through its fine gill rakers which sift out various types of microscopic plankton. Like other species of herring, Atlantic menhaden feed together in large, tight schools of similar sized fish as a means of protection. Unfortunately, these schools often attract the attention of predators such as seabirds and large toothy fish, particularly bluefish. And under certain circumstances, if a large school of menhaden is pushed into shallow enough water, it can trigger what is known as a "feeding frenzy." In a feeding frenzy, packs of bluefish rip into the defenseless school from below, while hordes of seagulls dive-bomb the school from above, creating a frothy fury of fins and feathers. Luckily, the schools are so large, up to thousands strong, that while many fish may be eaten, most will escape to swim another day. Menhaden can be found pretty much anywhere; large schools tend to be found in open water but often stray into the shallows. Unlike the alewife, the menhaden does not ascend rivers to spawn, it does, however, make seasonal migrations north to feed on plankton. They arrive in the Bay in the spring, feed until the fall, and return south for the winter.

Relationship to People: The Atlantic menhaden supports one of the largest commercial fisheries in Narragansett Bay. Interestingly, because their bodies are very oily, they are not harvested for food, rather they are used in soap, ink, pet feed, fertilizer, and for a variety of other industrial purposes. They are also important to recreational fishermen, as they are the preferred bait for several large game fish. Historically, overfishing has led to decreases in the menhaden population, fortunately new regulations are allowing populations to recover.

How to Find It: Menhaden are fairly common in Narragansett Bay, and can be found in most unpolluted areas, especially in autumn. Schools are easy to spot, and typically appear as a distinctive circle of ripples, with the occasional fin breaking the water's surface. Once a school is located, if the water is shallow enough, one can catch them using hand or seine nets. If the water is deeper, an effective method is to cast a treble hook into the school of fish and quickly reel in until one is snagged.

Baitfish
Atlantic Silverside *-Menidia menidia*
Other Names-silverside, spearing, baitfish, shiner, glass minnow

Habitat: It is common in most inshore waters, and often found along sandy beaches, in salt marsh creeks, amongst eelgrass beds, and in a variety of other coastal habitats.

Description: The Atlantic silverside is one of the most common and easily recognizable fish in Narragansett Bay. Overall, it is a translucent olive green color above, fading to a pale white color below, often times speckled with small dark dots. A bright silver stripe runs along the length of its body, hence the name, "silverside." There is also a silver-white patch, below the stripe, beginning behind its eye and extending to the base of its anal fin. The Atlantic silverside has a relatively small head, a blunt nose, and a small, upturned mouth. It has a small, rounded spiny dorsal fin, and a slightly larger, triangular soft dorsal fin, opposite a longer, straight-edged anal fin. The silverside has relatively large pectoral and pelvic fins and a slightly forked caudal fin. Its overall body shape is very long, slender, and slightly cylindrical. Silversides are fairly small fish, averaging 2-3 inches, but sometimes growing as large as 6 inches long.

Range: Outside of Narragansett Bay the Atlantic silverside can be found from the Gulf of St. Lawrence to Northeastern Florida. It is also present in Bermuda.

Behavior: The silverside has an omnivorous diet, and feeds readily on mysid shrimp, insect larvae, copepods, other kinds of zooplankton, and algae. They are in turn targeted by crabs, mantis shrimp, gulls, cormorants, and a host of larger species of fish, from summer flounder to northern sennet. Silversides tend to gather in large schools of similarly-sized fish, however, they don't school as tightly as other species like herring or butterfish. They swim high in the water column, often inches below the surface, where their planktonic prey is most abundant. Silversides are found very close to shore, often times in the company of other baitfish like killifish, menhaden, or anchovies. They are extremely common and can be found year-round, schooling along sandy beaches and mixed shoreline, amongst submerged vegetation, like eelgrass or saltmarsh chord-grass, and even in the brackish water of river mouths. Starting in early April, huge schools of silversides gather at the water's edge to begin spawning. At high tide, schools can be seen jumping into the air, writhing amongst the salt marsh grass, and even leaping onto rocks, all while releasing eggs and milt, in a wild mating display.

Relationship to People: As is the case with most small species of fish, the silverside is not harvested for consumption, but rather for use as bait. They are a common prey item for many kinds of fish, and are easily caught in large numbers, which makes them the perfect baitfish for recreational fishermen. They are also commonly used in scientific experiments, and can be kept for short periods of time in aquariums, (however, they aren't particularly interesting to look at, and usually die if kept too long).

How to Find It: Silversides rank with species like killifish and scup as some of the easiest fish to find in the Bay. They can be found pretty much anywhere and there are several ways one can catch them. Bait traps work well for those who are willing to wait half an hour or so; for more immediate gratification, large hand nets, seine nets, and cast nets are also effective. It is also possible to simply view silversides either from a dock, pier, or by snorkeling in shallow water.

Baitfish

Bay Anchovy - *Anchoa mitchilli*
Other Names - anchovy, common anchovy, glass minnow, fry, whitebait

Habitat: It prefers sandy or muddy bottoms near shore, although it is not particularly selective and is often found elsewhere. It also tolerates a wide range of salinities and can be found well into coastal rivers.

Description: The bay anchovy is mostly translucent, so when it is in the water it usually appears as a light bluish-green color. Like the silverside, it has a silver-white patch extending from behind its eye to the base of its anal fin, and a light silver stripe running laterally along the length of its body. It also has a series of black dots on the top of its head and along the base of its anal and caudal fins. The bay anchovy has a large diagonal scale pattern, often outlined in black; it also sometimes has a series of light orange dots running along its body. The major distinguishing feature of the bay anchovy is its wide mouth that extends well behind its very large eyes. Its pectoral and pelvic fins are both small, and its anal fin is relatively long and tapering. It has a deeply forked caudal fin and one soft dorsal fin located near the middle of its body. Its body shape is very elongate, and extremely horizontally compressed. It is a small fish, reaching a maximum of only 4 inches long.

Range: Outside of Narragansett Bay the bay anchovy can be found from the Gulf of Maine to Florida. It is also found throughout the Gulf of Mexico.

Behavior: As its small size would suggest, the bay anchovy is a filter feeder, using its large mouth full of tiny gill rakers to sift out microscopic plants and animals from the water. Where it is common, the anchovy represents an important link in the food chain, and is preyed upon by many species, including squid, crabs, wading birds, jellies, and many species of fish. The bay anchovy shares a similar ecological niche with the Atlantic silverside, thus the two species often compete and are not both common in the same immediate area. Like silversides, they are usually found in large loose schools of similarly-sized fish, often gathered just below the surface. They are less pollution-tolerant than silversides and tend to stay in the cleaner waters near the mouth of the Bay. They do, however, have a higher tolerance to changes in salinity, and are found well into freshwater. Bay anchovies tend to be found over sandy or muddy bottoms, although they are not particularly fastidious. They are most common in the Bay from mid-September to early October, but can be found in lesser numbers from May to early November.

Relationship to People: In certain parts of the world, anchovies are caught, canned, and sold for human consumption, however, their taste is debatable, and they are not particularly popular in the United States. Here, the most common use for them would be as chum or bait, (however, they are often too thin to stay on a hook). Bay anchovies are also popular research subjects for scientists studying estuarine health.

How to Find It: Although they share many of the same habits, anchovies are notably harder to find in Narragansett Bay than silversides, (they tend to be more common farther south, in states like New York or Maryland). Nevertheless, they can still be found in certain parts of the Bay at certain times during the year. The best places are in the southern part of the Bay, along sandy, protected shores; and the best times are in mid-September. To catch anchovies, simply look for large schools near the surface, and corral them with a seine net.

Baitfish

Rainbow Smelt -*Osmerus mordax*

Other Names-smelt, Atlantic smelt, salt-water smelt, arctic smelt

Habitat: It is always found within a mile of shore and in relatively shallow, cold water. During the autumn and winter months it enters harbors and estuaries and ascends coastal rivers, sometimes entering fresh water.

Description: The rainbow smelt is a dark olive-green color above, fading to a pale silvery-yellow color below. Along its midsection, there is a silvery-purple iridescent stripe, similar to that of the silverside, but less pronounced. Its fins are a light reddish-brown color. The smelt has a pointed snout, a large mouth filled with tiny teeth, and fairly large eyes. It has a medium-sized triangular soft dorsal fin located in the middle of its body, and a small but distinctive adipose fin located farther back. The rainbow smelt has a deeply forked caudal fin, and small anal and pelvic fins located just opposite the adipose and dorsal fins respectively. Its pectoral fins are small, triangular and transparent. The smelt's overall body shape is slender, elongated, and moderately compressed. It is larger than most other baitfish, growing up to 14 inches, but averages between 7 and 9 inches.

Range: Outside of Narragansett Bay the rainbow smelt ranges from Labrador to northern Virginia. It's also found in freshwater habitats throughout the region, as well as northern Alaska and part of northern Canada.

Behavior: Despite its rather small size, the rainbow smelt is an active predator. Juvenile smelt feed on zooplankton (predominately larval crustaceans), while adults feed on crustaceans like crabs, shrimp, and amphipods, as well as marine worms, small squid, insects, and fish like silversides, mummichogs, cunner, and sand lances. Smelt in turn are an important food source for several species of larger fish and seabirds. Like most other species of baitfish, the smelt has strong schooling tendencies, which aid in their search for food, and in protection against predators. Because it is pelagic, and almost always found at the surface or in the middle of the water column, the rainbow smelt shows no particular habitat preference based on bottom-type. Instead, its habitat is largely determined by temperature, with cold temperatures being preferable. During the summer they are found in deeper water, less than a mile offshore. In autumn they start moving into the shallows, gathering in harbors and bays, before entering into rivers where they overwinter and spawn. Rainbow smelt breed at night in the upper reaches of fresh or slightly brackish streams, in fa[st] moving, turbulent water, over rocks, bou[l]ders, and riverweed.

Relationship to People: Histo[ri]cally, the rainbow smelt supported a lucr[a]tive commercial fishery over much of [its] range. But since the beginning of the 20[th] century, the species has experienced lar[ge] declines due to overfishing and reduced w[a]tershed quality, and the commercial fishe[ry] has largely disappeared. In places whe[re] they're still common, smelt are actively pu[r]sued by recreational fishermen who targ[et] them in the winter for food.

How to Find It: Unfortunately, t[he] smelt is no longer present in the Bay in a[ny] great numbers, however, there are still ce[r]tain estuaries and rivers where they ca[n] sometimes be found. They are also mo[re] abundant in the winter, which likely discou[r]ages most people from pursuing them. Ne[v]ertheless, this is the best time to find the[m]. Smelt can be caught using light tackle, bait[ed] with clamworms, shrimp, or baitfish, on [a] mid-water rig. They're also sometim[es] caught with traps or seine nets.

Baitfish

American Sand Lance -*Ammodytes americanus*

Other Names-sand lance, sand eel, lancefish, lant

Habitat: It is typically found over sandy bottoms, both inshore off sandy beaches and on offshore banks.

Description: The American sand lance looks in many respects like a cross between a silverside and a small eel. It has an olive green back, purplish-blue iridescent sides, a white belly, and dusky brown fins. Sand lances have very small scales and their skin is very smooth to the touch. It has average-sized eyes, a fairly large head, and a sharply pointed snout. Its mouth is toothless, and it has a lower lip that extends slightly past the upper. The sand lance is unique in that it has one long soft dorsal fin, which extends along most of its body, and a similarly shaped anal fin which runs from the caudal fin to the middle of its body. It has small, sharply pointed pectoral fins, no pelvic fins, and a small forked caudal fin. Like an eel, its body is extremely slender, elongated, and somewhat rounded. Sand lances grow as large as 7 inches, but average just 3 to 4 inches long.

Range: Outside of Narragansett Bay the sand lance can be found from northern Labrador to Cape Hatteras, however, it is only common in the northern parts of its range.

Behavior: The American sand lance feeds on a variety of small marine animals, such as copepods, small crustaceans, fish fry, and marine worms. It plays an important ecological role in marine ecosystems, by serving as prey for everything from crabs and birds up to large fish and marine mammals. Of their many predators, it is their relationship with certain cetaceans that is most interesting. On offshore banks, humpback whales feed on vast numbers of sand lances using a unique tactic known as "bubble-netting." In this approach, the whales dive below a school of sand lances, surround them with a ring of carefully released bubbles (to confuse and entrap them), and then rush to the surface, mouth gaping wide, devouring as many fish as possible. This behavior would not be possible, were it not for the sand lances tendency to gather together in large dense schools of similarly-sized fish. When threatened, a sand lance will often dig itself several inches into the sand, leaving just its head exposed, and emerge only once it is sure the danger has passed. It is most common off shallow sandy beaches, but can be found in a wide range of depths. Sand lances spawn north of Narragansett Bay in early spring, and arrive in the Bay by early summer.

Relationship to People: The only direct use for the sand lance, recreationally or commercially, is as bait, and even so there are more popular alternatives. But because it supports the food chain for many species of fish, such as cod, pollock, and mackerel, all of which are commercially valuable, the sand lance has an indirect yet still powerful significance to people.

How to Find It: The American sand lance is more common north of the Bay, and is more likely to be encountered in Massachusetts or Maine than in Rhode Island. Nevertheless, it is occasionally found in this area. The best places to look are off sandy beaches near the mouth of the Bay. They swim together in large schools, and look very similar to silversides when viewed from above, so one must actually catch one to know for sure that it is a sand lance. The most effective way to catch them is to use a seine net, but hand nets can also work.

Butterfish - *Peprilus triacanthus*

Other Names—American butterfish, shiner, dollarfish, butters, harvestfish

Habitat: It is almost always found over sandy bottoms in areas of high salinity, and can be found both inshore in protected bays and estuaries, and offshore in relatively deep water.

Description: The butterfish has a grayish-blue back, iridescent silver sides marked with darker spots and purplish-pink hues, and a shiny white belly. Its fins range from a light yellowish brown to dark slate gray color. Its skin is very smooth, and it has small scales which rub off easily when touched. The butterfish has large eyes, a blunt snout, and a small, upturned mouth with tiny teeth. It has a deeply forked caudal fin, long pointed pectoral fins, and no pelvic fins. It has one long soft dorsal fin, which slowly tapers towards the tail, and a slightly shorter anal fin directly below it. The most distinctive feature of the butterfish is its body shape, which is very deep, rounded, and extremely horizontally compressed. (In fact, young fish are often so thin that, when viewed from above, they are almost impossible to see). Butterfish grow larger than most other baitfish, averaging 4 to 6 inches long, but sometimes grow as large as 12 inches.

Range: Outside of Narragansett Bay the butterfish is found from Newfoundland to Florida, and is more common in the northern part of its range.

Behavior: The butterfish feeds primarily on small soft-bodied prey items, like tunicates, ctenophores, jellies, annelids, and juvenile fish and squid. Like most other species of baitfish, it is preyed upon by a range of larger fish, such as bluefish, weakfish, and several species of tuna. To protect themselves, adult butterfish often travel together in medium-sized schools just below the surface. Juvenile butterfish, which are more solitary early on in life, find protection amongst the stinging tentacles of jellies, such as sea nettles and lion's manes, to whose venom they are apparently immune. This association is not essential to the butterfish's well-being, however, as young fish are also often observed swimming independently. Schools of butterfish can be found both close to shore and in water several hundreds of feet deep, and are frequently encountered in the same habitat as the longfin inshore squid (*Doryteuthis pealeii*). They have a strict preference for areas with sandy bottoms and high salinity, and are rarely, if ever, found in brackish water, or over rock and mud. The butterfish is found in Narragansett Bay starting in late April, it spawns during mid-summer, and migrates south and offshore by November.

Relationship to People: Despite its relatively small size, the butterfish supports a valuable yet currently under-fished commercial fishery in Rhode Island. Although it is very oily, it is still delicious, highly underrated, and makes fine table fare. They are also caught recreationally, sometimes for food, but more often as chum bait for larger game fish, especially tuna.

How to Find It: For the average person, the butterfish is surprisingly hard to find in Narragansett Bay. Scientists and commercial fishermen often catch them in great numbers using otter trawls, but for the average fish enthusiast, finding one is notably more difficult, (at least in the Bay). Nevertheless, there are things one can do to improve their chances of finding one. Butterfish prefer areas with high salinity, so water near the mouth of the Bay are ideal; they also have a strict preference for sandy bottoms. They can be caught on light tackle, but the best way to catch them is with nets.

Baitfish

American Eel - *Anguilla rostrata*

Other Names - common eel, silver eel, freshwater eel, eel

Habitat: It can be found in a wide range of saltwater and freshwater habitats, especially in muddy estuaries and river mouths, but it is not picky and can be found almost anywhere.

Description: The American eel is a dark shiny black color over much of its body, fading to greenish yellow on its sides and eventually to a creamy white belly, although juveniles may be a lime-green color over their entire bodies. Its pectoral fins are usually a dusky brown color. Morphologically, the American eel has very distinctive features, and is fairly easy to identify, (although young ones could be confused with rock gunnels). It has very small, barely distinguishable scales, and is covered in a thick layer of slime. The American eel has a large head with long jaws, a pointed snout, and two medium sized eyes. It has rounded pectoral fins, no pelvic fins, and its dorsal, caudal, and anal fins are all fused together into a long paddle-like tail. Its overall body shape is extremely elongate and cylindrical, so much so that this fish is sometimes confused with a snake. The American eel can grow to nearly five feet long, but is usually much smaller, averaging up to 18 inches.

Range: Outside of Narragansett Bay the American eel can be found from Labrador to Guyana. It is also found in the Gulf of Mexico, and in many freshwater locales, from the Great Lakes to the Missouri River.

Behavior: The American eel is omnivorous and has an extremely varied diet. In freshwater, eels eat fish, frogs, worms, and insects, while in saltwater they prey upon crabs, clams, shrimp, and detritus. They are in turn preyed upon by sea birds such as gulls and ospreys, and large fish, especially the striped bass. Eels are largely nocturnal, spending their days resting and nights hunting. They tend to live in protected harbors, muddy estuaries, and river mouths, although they aren't especially picky and can be found nearly anywhere, provided there is enough prey. The American eel is catadromous, meaning it spends most of its life in freshwater and migrates into to saltwater to spawn. In many ways the life cycle of an eel is the reverse of that of a salmon. For most of their lives, eels live and grow in the fresh and brackish waters of coastal rivers. In early fall, adults cease feeding, leave freshwater, and enter Narragansett Bay on their migration south to spawn. From here, the eels continue southward to the Sargasso Sea off Bermuda. By midwinter, all adults have finished spawning and died. Juvenile eels develop offshore for about a year, before returning to the coastal rivers to begin the cycle anew.

Relationship to People: In the Bay, the American eel is primarily used as bait, as it is the preferred method for catching large striped bass, (it works well in catching bluefish as well). Historically, eels have also supported significant commercial fisheries, as they are a prized food fish in many Asian cultures and often used in sushi. This pressure has taken its toll, however, and populations are now relatively low.

How to Find It: The American eel is not abundant in Narragansett Bay, but thanks to its predictable annual behavior, it is easy to find, if one knows how. The best times to catch them are when juveniles return from the sea, from mid-May to early June, or when adults leave the rivers to spawn, from late September to mid-October. Most places will work, but those with muddy bottoms seem to be preferable. They can be caught with nets and fishing rods, but the most efficient method is a simple bait trap.

Part 2:
Tropical Strays

Jacks

Bigeye Scad - *Selar crumenophthalmus*

Other Names - goggle-eye scad, goggle-eye jack, goggler

Habitat: It is typically found in shallow coastal areas, often in turbid water and amongst eelgrass beds.

Description: The bigeye scad is characterized by a metallic purplish-blue to reddish-bronze color above, transitioning to a light silvery-white below; its fins are a translucent tannish-green color. Often times it is also adorned with several small black spots scattered haphazardly over its body. One interesting feature of the bigeye scad, also shared by many other species in the Jack family), is the presence of a series of eel-like scutes along its lateral line, although in this species they are only present on the rear half of the line. It has a relatively large mouth and, as its name suggests, disproportionately large eyes. It has a deeply forked caudal fin and falcate pectoral fins. The bigeye scad has one small, triangular spiny dorsal fin, and one long, tapering soft dorsal fin, reflected below by a shorter, similarly shaped anal fin. It has a fusiform, moderately elongate body and is horizontally compressed. It can grows up to a foot long, but averages between 4 and 6 inches.

Range: Outside of Narragansett Bay the bigeye scad is found in the western Atlantic from Nova Scotia to Brazil, and is more common in the southern part of its range. It is also found in other tropical and temperate waters worldwide.

Behavior: The bigeye scad feeds entirely on pelagic prey; juveniles target invertebrates, such as shrimp and crab larvae, and adults consume small fish such as silversides and anchovies. In other parts of its range, the bigeye scad is preyed upon by large game species such as tuna and billfish, however in Rhode Island, it is more likely to be eaten by species like bluefish or striped bass. The bigeye scad is a fast, schooling fish, sometimes found in groups of hundreds or even thousands, although here in the Bay they are usually encountered roaming in groups of just three or four. As its abnormally large eyes suggest, the bigeye scad is a predominantly nocturnal predator, and almost never feeds during the day. Since it is a pelagic species, and usually remains near the surface of the water column, it has no real habitat preferences, although it is often found alongside other tropical strays in large eelgrass beds. It is one of the most common tropical strays in the Bay, and one of the first to arrive. It can be found starting in early June, and remains until late August.

Relationship to People: The bigeye scad is occasionally caught by recreational fisherman for food, but due to its small size, most people use it as bait. In the southern part of its range, it is commonly used to catch offshore species like tuna and sailfish, and it also supports a meager commercial fishery. Conceivably, juvenile scad could also be kept in aquaria.

How to Find It: Compared to most native species, the bigeye scad is relatively rare, but compared to other tropical strays, it is practically abundant. It is often found in protected eelgrass beds, but since it has no distinct habitat preferences, it could show up just about anywhere. The bigeye scad is a notoriously fast fish, so hand nets and slurp guns are usually ineffective. Cast nets and light tackle angling could work, however, the most effective way to catch one is a large seine net, which when used correctly even the bigeye scad cannot escape.

Crevalle Jack - *Caranx hippos*

Other Names - crevalle, jack crevalle, jack, hardtail, common jackfish

Habitat: It is found in protected inshore waters, along sandy beaches, over muddy bottoms, and in eelgrass beds.

Description: The crevalle jack is typically olive green to dark blue above with whitish-silver sides; however, some young fish can be greenish-yellow or even gold in color. In addition, juveniles typically have 5 or 6 dark vertical bars. Most of its fins are an orange-yellow color, and its dorsal fin is often edged in black. The crevalle is distinguished from other jacks by its large eyes, blunt snout, deeply curved forehead, and large mouth. Its lateral line is arched, and it has several keeled scutes along its caudal peduncle. This jack has one well-developed, triangular spiny dorsal fin, and one longer, tapering soft dorsal fin. Its anal fin is similar to its second dorsal fin, it has scimitar-shaped pectoral fins, rounded pelvic fins, and a deeply forked caudal fin. The jack's overall body shape is oblong, robust and compressed. Crevalle jacks can grow over 3 feet long, and over 50 pounds, but in the Bay they're rarely larger than 10 inches.

Similar Species: The yellow jack (*Caranx bartholomaei*) is another species, similar to the crevalle that is also occasionally found in the Bay. The yellow jack is more streamlined than the crevalle, its forehead isn't as steep, and it is more brightly patterned. Its habits are similar to those of the crevalle, and it is rarer in Narragansett Bay.

Range: Outside of Narragansett Bay the crevalle jack is found from Nova Scotia to Uruguay, including the Gulf of Mexico, Caribbean, and parts of the Eastern Atlantic.

Behavior: The crevalle jack is in many respects, "the bluefish of the south." This is because it is a fast, active predator that greedily feeds on schools of baitfish, and is found in a wide range of habitats. Consequently, the juvenile crevalles found in Narragansett Bay are similar to young, "snapper" bluefish. These juvenile jacks feed primarily on small baitfish, such as anchovies, silversides, and menhaden, as well as shrimp, and other invertebrates. They are in turn preyed upon by other finfish, such as bluefish and striped bass, (farther south, they are eaten by larger species, such as striped marlin and goliath grouper). Juvenile crevalles are strict schooling fish, and roam together in fast, active groups, cooperatively hunting by corralling baitfish into tight balls. As they grow larger, however, crevalles become more solitary and tend to hunt alone. The crevalle jack is found mid-water over sand and mud bottoms, as well as in eelgrass beds. It is found in the Bay from late June to mid-September.

Relationship to People: The crevalle jack has a particularly unappetizing flavor, and thus only supports a small commercial fishery in the southern part of its range. It does, however, have a strong, dogged fighting style, and is popular with recreational sport fishermen. Unfortunately, in Rhode Island they don't get large enough to support any fisheries, except for use as bait.

How to Find It: Like all tropical strays, the crevalle jack is not *abundant* in Narragansett Bay, however, it is one of the most common species found here. They can be found nearly anywhere, although eelgrass beds and protected areas over sand or mud bottoms are the best places to look. They can be caught the same way one catches juvenile bluefish: either angling with light tackle or using a large seine net.

Jacks

Permit - *Trachinotus flacatus*
Other Names - round pompano, great pompano, cobbler

Habitat: It is found along protected shallow beaches, often among seaweed, and in healthy eelgrass beds.

Description: The permit is usually a silvery-white color over most of its body, with a slight bluish-green tinge above, although some juveniles are a dark, grayish-black color, which can be difficult to identify. In juveniles, the dorsal fins are typically dark black, the anal fin is reddish orange, and the eyes are ruby red. The permit has fairly large eyes, a blunt snout, and a soft, fleshy mouth. It has one spiny dorsal fin consisting of six prominent spines, immediately followed by an elongated and tapering soft dorsal fin. Its anal fin is similar to its second dorsal fin, it has small triangular pelvic fins, medium-sized pectoral fins, and a deeply forked caudal fin. The permit's overall body shape is rounded, deep, and quite compressed. It can grow as large as 56 pounds, and over 3 feet long, however, only juveniles are found in the Bay, and they rarely grow over 2 inches.

Similar Species: The Florida pompano (*Trachinotus carolinus*) is another species of jack, closely related to the permit, that is also occasionally found in Narragansett Bay. The pompano has a more oblong body shape than the permit, and a broader caudal fin as well. It is a light olive green color above, with silvery sides, and is a distinct golden-yellow color on its belly, pelvic, and anal fins.

Range: Outside of Narragansett Bay the permit is found from Massachusetts to Brazil, as well as the Caribbean and Gulf of Mexico.

Behavior: As is the case with most tropical strays, the lifestyles of juvenile and adult permit are quite different. Adults feed on invertebrates such as shrimps, crabs, barnacles, urchins, and mollusks, while juveniles consume species like amphipods, copepods, mysid shrimp, and small marine worms. Because of their size, juveniles are vulnerable to any carnivore larger than they are. Adults on the other hand, are only susceptible to large predators such as sharks and barracudas. Juvenile permit, such as those found in Narragansett Bay, are solitary, weak swimmers, and tend to stay near the bottom, hiding amongst eelgrass, and other aquatic debris. As they grow larger, they become stronger, more active swimmers, and roam in small schools when hunting for prey. A juvenile permit's habitat is largely determined by currents and wind direction. Farther south they tend to settle on the windward side of sandy beaches, but in Narragansett Bay they are usually found in large eelgrass beds. The permit is found in the Bay from July until early October.

Relationship to People: The permit makes fine table fare, and supports a modest commercial fishery in the Gulf region, where it is managed together with the Florida pompano. It is also a popular target for recreation anglers in Florida and the Gulf States, especially amongst fly fishermen, who appreciate its wily nature and superior fighting abilities. In the Bay, juveniles are sometimes caught and kept in aquaria.

How to Find It: Permit are fairly uncommon in the Bay, nevertheless a few are caught at certain locales each year. The best places to look are protected eelgrass beds and areas where aquatic debris washes up. Starting in late July, they can be caught by snorkeling with a slurp gun, setting a bait trap, or even throwing a cast net, although seining is the most efficient method.

Jacks
Atlantic Moonfish -*Selene setapinnis*

Other Names-moonfish, dollarfish, lookdown, flatjack, horsefish, bluntnose,

Habitat: It can be found in coastal areas with sandy and muddy bottoms such as estuaries and river mouths. It also inhabits deeper water, and is sometimes found around buoys and navigation markers.

Description: The Atlantic moonfish is a lustrous silver color over most of its body, complemented by light iridescent hues, and a pale bluish green tinge above. Juveniles have a dark black streak above their eyes, a small black oval over their lateral lines, and pale greenish-brown fins. It has small, fine scales, medium sized eyes and a terminal mouth. The most distinctive feature of the moonfish is certainly its extremely steep (almost vertical) and slightly concave head profile. It has four short, separated spines, in front of a long, tapering, soft dorsal fin, mirrored below by a slightly smaller, yet similarly shaped anal fin. It has falcate pectoral fins, miniscule pelvic fins, and a deeply forked caudal fin. The Atlantic moonfish has an extremely deep, very thin, oval-shaped body, with a narrow caudal peduncle. In the southern part of its range it can grow as large as 13 inches, but in Rhode Island it rarely grows past 4 inches.

Similar Species: Surprisingly, the Atlantic moonfish is not the goofiest looking fish in Narragansett Bay. This distinction goes to its close relative the lookdown (*Selene vomer*), another species of jack occasionally found in late summer. The lookdown has an even steeper head profile, a less elongate body shape, and elongated first rays of its dorsal and anal fins.

Range: Outside of Narragansett Bay the Atlantic moonfish is found from Nova Scotia to Argentina, including most of the Caribbean Sea and the Gulf of Mexico.

Behavior: The Atlantic moonfish is an efficient predator and feeds on a range of small fish, marine worms, and crustaceans. Because adults only grow to about a foot long, they are susceptible to predation by a wide range of species, including barracuda, snook, and larger jacks; the juveniles found in the Bay are at risk from bluefish, striped bass, and bonitos. Fortunately, the moonfish, with its ultra-thin body and deeply forked caudal fin, is highly maneuverable and fast enough to escape all but the most skilled predators. This speed and agility is also useful during feeding, when large schools of moonfish patrol above the sea floor in search of prey. However, only adult moonfish live near the sea floor; juveniles tend to school near the surface. The Atlantic moonfish is not particularly fastidious with its habitat preferences, although it is usually found over sandy or muddy bottoms, often in estuaries and around pilings or buoys. Moonfish first appear in the Bay in late August and remain here until early October.

Relationship to People: Due to its thin body, the Atlantic moonfish is not a common food fish in most of North America, however, in certain parts of the Caribbean it does support a small commercial fishery. Eating moonfish is risky, however, considering this species has been known to carry ciguatera poisoning. In the Bay, a more common use for a moonfish would be as a curiosity in an amateur's aquarium.

How to Find It: The Atlantic moonfish is relatively common in the Bay, and for the past few years, as water temperatures have increased, their numbers have steadily grown. Unfortunately most of these fish are caught by bottom trawling, a method inaccessible to most people. For those without this option, the best plan is seining along sandy beaches near the mouth of the Bay.

Puffers and Boxfishes

Bandtail Puffer - *Sphoeroides spengleri*

Other Names - southern swellfish

Habitat: It is found in shallow eelgrass beds and on the margins of coral and rocky reefs.

Description: The banded puffer is an olive green to tannish grey color above, fading to a light yellowish bronze, and eventually a creamy white belly. As its name suggests, its tail is marked with two black bands, and along the bronze margins of each side it has a distinct row of black spots. Along its back and sides, it also has several white, fleshy flaps of skin. It has fairly large eyes situated at the top of its head, and a small mouth with beak-like jaws. Like the northern puffer, the bandtail puffer has one small pointed soft dorsal fin located far back on its body, and a nearly identical anal fin. Its pectoral fins are rounded, its caudal fin is truncate, and it has no pelvic fins. Its body shape is elongate, and somewhat boxy, and like other puffers it becomes globular in shape when disturbed. The bandtail puffer is small, growing to only 7 inches long; those in the Bay are usually less than an inch.

Similar Species: The striped burrfish (*Chilomycterus schoepfi*) is another puffer occasionally found in the Bay. It is different from the northern and bandtail puffers in that its body is covered with a series of sharp spines that are erect even when the fish is uninflated. It is more boxlike in shape, and is a yellowish brown color, covered with black lines and a few black blotches.

Range: Outside of Narragansett Bay the bandtail puffer is found from Massachusetts to Brazil, including the Gulf of Mexico and Caribbean Sea.

Behavior: The bandtail puffer is omnivorous, feeding on several kinds of crustaceans, mollusks, worms, echinoderms, algae, and seagrass. Their small size makes them vulnerable to reef predators such as lizardfish, eels, and groupers, although they have several means of defense. Bandtail puffers are typically found in the shallow water of reefs and seagrass beds, providing them with ample places to hide. Like the northern puffer, they also possess the ability to inflate themselves with water when threatened, making them difficult to swallow. But unlike the northern puffer, the bandtail puffer is actually poisonous, and contains both saxitoxins and tetrodotoxins, powerful neurotoxins that, in humans, can cause numbness, nausea, vomiting, seizure, paralysis, and in rare cases, death. Unsurprisingly, most predators tend to avoid this species. The bandtail puffer is a solitary, bottom-dwelling species usually seen hovering above the sea floor, or darting around looking for food. They arrive in the Bay in mid-July and stay until late September.

Relationship to People: Considering its small size, and inherent toxicity, it's no surprise that there is no recreational or commercial fishery for the bandtail puffer. There only significant use is in the aquarium trade, and even so, they are usually not commercially available.

How to Find It: The bandtail puffer is one of the more common tropicals in Narragansett Bay. They are found among shallow rocky areas and in large eelgrass beds, often alongside juvenile northern puffers. They can be caught using several different methods. Seine nets are the most efficient, but only in areas without large rocks. Snorkeling with hand nets also works well, although they can be difficult to spot, and are sometimes confused with northern puffers.

Puffers and Boxfishes

Trunkfish -*Lactophrys trigonus*

Other Names-common trunkfish, buffalo trunkfish, boxfish

Habitat: It is almost always found in shallow eelgrass beds.

Description: Juvenile trunkfish are highly variable in color, and can appear in various shades of black, brown, green, or yellow, with overlying spots and blotches. Although they still vary somewhat in color, adults are typically greenish brown, with a series of small white spots, dark brown blotches, and a white belly. It has large eyes, a deeply sloping head, and a pointed snout with a small mouth. The trunkfish has one soft, rounded dorsal fin located at the beginning of its caudal peduncle, and a similar anal fin directly below. It has a rounded caudal fin (which can be difficult to see in juveniles), large pectoral fins, and no pelvic fins. The body shape of the trunkfish is arguably the most unusual of any fish in the Bay. It is closest to that of a puffer, box-like with a roughly triangular cross section, a high arch in its back, and two rear facing spines below. Unlike most fish, its body is rigid, and shell-like, formed by a series of hexagonal plates known as a cuirass. It grows fairly large, up to 18 inches long, although those found in the Bay are extremely small, often no larger than a pea.

Range: Outside of Narragansett Bay the trunkfish can be found from Massachusetts to Brazil, as well as the Gulf of Mexico and Caribbean Sea.

Behavior: The trunkfish feeds on several kinds of small benthic organisms, including worms, crustaceans, mollusks, and tunicates. Their relatively small size puts them at risk from predators such as moray eels, groupers, and nurse sharks, although they are not popular prey. Most predators find their rigid, bulky bodies unappetizing, and downright difficult to consume. And if they are attacked, trunkfish can also secrete an agent known as pahutoxin, a substance capable of killing other fish, even ones much larger than them. So like the bandtail puffer, trunkfish are largely left alone to do as they please. This is especially fortunate for the trunkfish as they are slow, clumsy swimmers, capable of only short bursts of speed. They spend most of their time roaming around shallow sea grass beds and the edges of reefs in search of food. In many ways, trunkfish can be thought of as the smaller, slower, piscine equivalent to sea turtles. Trunkfish spawn in the spring, and are one of the later tropicals to appear, arriving in early August and staying until the end of September.

Relationship to People: Despite its relatively small size, and awkward appearance, the trunkfish does support a minor artisanal fishery in many Caribbean islands although in the southern United States they are only regarded as bait stealers. They are potentially valuable in the aquarium trade although the toxins they excrete when under distress can be dangerous to other fish.

How to Find It: The trunkfish is fairly rare in Narragansett Bay, although this may partially be due to its extremely small size. The juveniles found in the Bay are so small, rarely over half an inch long, that they often go unnoticed by even the most watchful eyes. Consequently, snorkeling with a net or slurp gun rarely turns up anything, unless one is very experienced. Seining is definitely the best option, but one still has to look hard to spot this tiny, pea-sized fish. Eelgrass beds near the mouth of the Bay are the best places to look for them.

Colorful Deep-Bodied Tropicals
Spotfin Butterflyfish -*Chaetodon ocellatus*
Other Names-butterflyfish, common butterflyfish, butterfly, parche

Habitat: It is found in shallow rocky areas, in cracks and crevices, and amongst seaweed. Adults are found on coral and rocky reefs.

Description: The spotfin butterflyfish is certainly one of the most visually striking and iconic tropical strays found in the Bay. In juveniles, the body can be anything from a bright white to a slate grey color, depending on the environment. It also has two vertical black bands, one running through the eyes, and one running from the anal fin to the soft portion of the dorsal fin. The dorsal, pelvic, and part of the anal fins are a vibrant yellow color, and the tail is transparent. In adults, the black band between the dorsal and anal fins disappears, all of the fins become bright yellow, and there is typically a black spot on the edge of the soft dorsal fin. The butterflyfish has large eyes, a small pointed mouth, and a slightly concave head profile in front of its snout. It has one continuous dorsal fin, with a higher spiny portion, and a lower soft portion. Its anal fin is roughly the same size and shape as the soft dorsal fin, its pelvic fins are fairly large and pointed, and it has a truncate caudal fin. The spotfin butterflyfish has a very deep, compressed, disk-like body shape. It can grow up to 8 inches, but those found in the Bay are rarely more than an inch long.

Range: Outside of Narragansett Bay the spotfin butterflyfish is found from Massachusetts to Brazil, including the Gulf of Mexico and the Caribbean Sea.

Behavior: The spotfin butterflyfish is a delicate fish that uses its tiny mouth to feed on invertebrates such as tunicates, polychaete worms, gorgonians, and zoanthids. Adults are vulnerable to a variety of tropical predators, such as snappers, groupers, moray eels, and barracudas; the juveniles found in the Bay are potential prey for nearly any carnivorous fish more than a few inches in length. Because they are so vulnerable, juvenile butterflyfish spend the majority of their time hiding. They are fairly territorial, and once they have chosen a suitable coral head or rock ledge, they tend to not stray very far. Despite their inherent vulnerability, they are still very curious, and will cautiously come out to investigate if a snorkeler or diver approaches. Adult butterflyfish, while bolder than juveniles, still remain in a relatively small portion of reef for most of their lives, and spend most of their time foraging near the bottom. Butterflyfish usually travel in pairs of one female and one male, and unlike most fish, they typically mate for life.

Relationship to People: The spotfin butterflyfish is too small to be targeted for human consumption, but its bright colors and active personality make it popular in the aquarium trade. In fact, no other species in the Bay garners as much attention from amateur aquarists looking to add to their collections as the spotfin butterflyfish.

How to Find It: The spotfin butterflyfish is certainly the most common tropical species found in the Bay, and can be consistently found every year. Nevertheless, they can be difficult to catch if one doesn't know the proper techniques. Their rocky habitat makes the use of seine nets effectively impossible, and their small size clearly rules out traditional angling. Bait traps would probably work, but the best method is snorkeling with a hand net or slurp gun. It takes a sharp eye to spot a dime-sized butterflyfish hiding beneath a rocky ledge, but after it is found, it is fairly easy to either slurp it up, or gently coax it into a net.

Colorful Deep-Bodied Tropicals

Short Bigeye -*Pristigenys alta*

Other Names-deep bigeye, bigeye

Habitat: It is found over rocky bottoms, in burrows, and under ledges. Adults live in water a few hundred feet deep.

Description: The short bigeye is easily distinguished from any other Narragansett Bay species by its vibrant, neon red coloration. In juveniles, the ventral and anal fins are black with white speckles, its caudal fin is transparent, and the dorsal fin is white with red spots. In adults, all the fins are pale red, sometimes edged in black. One of the short bigeye's most distinctive features are its eyes, which are not only very large, but also have special reflective lenses that glow when photographed with a flash. The short bigeye has a large, upturned mouth, and a lower jaw that extends past the upper. It has one continuous dorsal fin, with a high, pointed soft portion, and a spiny portion composed of 10 sharp, stout spines. Its anal fin is similar in size and form to the soft dorsal, its caudal fin is square-shaped and slightly convex, and its ventral fins are very large and rounded. The short bigeye has a deep, (nearly circular), horizontally compressed body. It grows to a maximum of 10 inches long, but those found in the Bay are around 1 inch long.

Range: Outside of Narragansett Bay the short bigeye is found from Maine to northern South America, including the Gulf of Mexico and the Caribbean Sea.

Behavior: The short bigeye is a crafty ambush predator that feeds mainly on smaller species of fish. It hunts by hiding beneath a rocky ledge until something passes by, and then rushing up from below and seizing the unsuspecting prey in its distinctly upturned mouth. In fact, it is so specialized in this method of hunting, that if the prey escapes and ends up below the bigeye, the shape of its mouth makes it impossible to make another strike without first repositioning beneath the prey. It is a solitary nocturnal fish that, even as an adult, spends most of its time hiding in burrows and under ledges over rocky bottoms. This secretive lifestyle protects the short bigeye from being detected by most species, yet this fish has another, less obvious form of protection. In the deep water where adults are usually found, the red portion of the light spectrum quickly disappears, (eventually so do all the other colors). And so the bright red coloration that makes juveniles so conspicuous in the shallows during the day, makes the same fish practically invisible at night in deep water. Juvenile sho bigeye are found in the Bay from late July September.

Relationship to People: Like t spotfin butterflyfish, the short bigeye is t small to be caught commercially or recre tionally as a food or game fish, and so i main value is as part of the aquarium trad Yet it is still relatively rare, and is not con monly bought or sold like the spotfin butte flyfish. Those found in aquaria are likely t result of personal collecting.

How to Find It: Although the short bi eye is relatively rare in Narragansett Bay, is still a fairly iconic tropical stray. Like t butterflyfish, the short bigeye's rocky habit makes snorkeling with a hand net or slu gun the only viable targeting method. Th can be overkill, however, considering sho bigeyes sleep during the day, and are so i active that they can literally be picked up i one's hand. (Although a net is still more r liable). The difficulty is finding them, sinc they aren't very common and like to hide i burrows and under ledges.

Colorful Deep-Bodied Tropicals
Planehead Filefish - *Stephanolepis hispidus*
Other Names - common filefish, green filefish, filefish, foolfish

Habitat: It is found in a wide range of habitats, but prefers sandy or muddy bottoms and eelgrass beds. It also lives offshore amongst sargassum weed, and is often blown inshore.

Description: The planehead filefish ranges in color from a light green to a dark brown, often overlaid with dark blotches or spots. The filefish gets its name from its skin, which is very rough, sandpapery, and file-like. It has a pointed, angular head, with a small terminal mouth filled with sharp incisor-like teeth. It has one long dorsal spine that it can erect at will, and a long, rounded soft dorsal fin, mirrored below by a nearly identical anal fin. Its caudal fin is wide and unlike, its pectoral fins are short and rounded, and instead of pelvic fins, it has a long pelvic spine which it can move to make its body appear deeper. Its overall body shape is deep, angular, and somewhat diamond-shaped. It is fairly small, growing to only 10 inches long, although those found in the Bay are usually only 1-4 inches.

Similar Species: The orange filefish (*Aluterus schoepfii*) is another species sometimes found in Narragansett Bay. It grows larger than the planehead filefish, up to 2 feet in length, and its body is more elongated and oblong. It is usually orange brown in color, and often has darker mottling as well. Its habitat and behavior are fairly similar to those of the planehead filefish.

Range: Outside of Narragansett Bay the planehead filefish is found Nova Scotia to Brazil, including the Gulf of Mexico and Caribbean Sea. It is also present in the Eastern Atlantic from the Canary Islands to Angola.

Behavior: The filefish is an omnivore, feeding on tunicates, crustaceans, worms, urchins, fish eggs, seagrass, and several kinds of algae. It is in turn consumed by larger fish such as tunas, dolphinfish, and bluefish as well as seabirds such as cormorants and petrels. It is a fairly docile, shy species that is usually seen either hovering motionless among floating weeds or slowly cruising along the bottom, picking around for food. When a predator attacks, the planehead filefish attempts to escape by swimming into a crevice, and erecting its dorsal and pelvic spines, thereby safely wedging itself inside its rocky shelter until the threat has disappeared. Planehead filefish can be found in a wide variety of habitats, but are usually associated with sand or mud bottoms and seagrass beds. They are also commonly found far offshore amongst sargassum weed, and often get blown into the shallow waters of the Bay after large storms. They're one of the first tropicals to appear in the Bay and one of the last to die off, arriving as early as mid-June, and staying until mid-October.

Relationship to People: The planehead filefish is considered by most fisherman in the United States to be too small and unappetizing to be worth targeting. In other parts of the world, however, they are caught commercially and have even experienced overfishing. Filefish are also valuable in the aquarium trade, although they are known to sometimes damage corals and other invertebrates.

How to Find It: The planehead filefish is fairly common in Narragansett Bay, especially after large storms. They are typically found near the mouth of the Bay, in places where storm debris washes up, especially if these places also have large eelgrass beds and sandy bottoms. They can be observed and caught by snorkeling, although the best way to catch them is using a large seine net.

Colorful Deep-Bodied Tropicals

Pinfish -*Lagodon rhomboides*

Other Names-pin perch, shiner, Spanish porgy, sailors' choice, bream

Habitat: It is found close to shore in eelgrass beds, salt marshes, and among aquatic vegetation. Larger ones are found in deeper water around holes and other structure.

Description: The pinfish has a light silvery sheen overall, permeated by a series of yellowish bronze and light blue horizontal stripes. On top of this it has several vertical, dusky brown saddles, and its most distinguishing feature, a dark shoulder spot centered on its lateral line. Its eyes and mouth are average in size, it has a short, somewhat pointed snout, and its head profile is more gently sloping than that of the scup, (a closely related member of the porgy family). The pinfish has one long continuous dorsal fin, with a soft and spiny portion, and a long, rectangular anal fin. Its pectoral and pelvic fins are fairly large and pointed, and its caudal fin is moderately forked. Its overall body shape is laterally compressed, oblong, and fairly deep, although not as deep as the scup. It grows to a maximum of about 15 inches and a few pounds, but those found in the Bay are usually 1-4 inches.

Similar Species: The spottail pinfish (*Diplodus holbrooki*) and the sheepshead (*Archosargus probatocephalus*) are two other tropical porgies occasionally found in the Bay. The spottail pinfish is a dusky silver color over most of its body with a distinctive black saddle on its caudal peduncle, and the sheepshead is a dirty white color with 5-6 thick black bars running vertically across its entire body.

Range: Outside of Narragansett Bay the pinfish is found from Cape Cod to the Yucatan Peninsula, as well as the Gulf of Mexico.

Behavior: The pinfish is an omnivorous species, feeding on a variety of fish eggs, shrimp, worms, amphipods, isopods, seagrass, and algae. It is in turn a vitally important prey species for dozens of southern predators, such as sea trout, snappers, groupers, redfish, egrets, pelicans, and bottlenose dolphins. Juvenile pinfish are commonly found in shallow seagrass beds, salt marshes, and mangroves, all of which provide abundant cover to conceal them from predators. They are a fairly active, diurnal fish, and while they do not school together, they can often be found in large aggregations foraging near the bottom, all within a relatively small local area. As pinfish grow larger, and the threat from predators decreases, they are emboldened to move to deeper areas where they congregate around holes and other structures. In the fall and winter, pinfish move offshore to spawn, and their offspring are some of the first tropical strays to arrive the Bay, coming as early as mid-June, and staying until mid-October.

Relationship to People: Although the pinfish is usually considered too small eat, it is still incredibly important, commercially and recreationally, as a bait and forage fish. Dozens of large predatory game fish, including snook, drums, groupers, and jack all rely on the pinfish for food, and pinfish are commonly used in the southeastern United States for bait. Large pinfish can be caught on light tackle, and even make fine eating, although most anglers only see the bait value.

How to Find It: The pinfish is one of the more common strays in Narragansett Bay, and one of the first found each year. They are common in eelgrass beds, although salt marshes and sandy beaches with seaweed will likely have them as well. "Pinfish traps" are the best way to catch them in the South, but in the Bay, seine nets are better.

Colorful Deep-Bodied Tropicals

Scamp -*Mycteroperca phenax*
Other Names-scamp grouper, brown grouper, broomtail grouper

Habitat: It is typically found in rocky areas, often hiding in holes and crevices. Adults are found offshore on deep reefs.

Description: The scamp is a light pinkish tan color overall, with a series of darker spots clustered into blotches and lines, often forming a reticulated pattern. Its fins are often patterned as well, and juveniles have a lighter area around the belly in front of the anal fin. It has a large gently-sloping head, with large eyes, a wide, slightly oblique mouth, and a lower jaw that extends slightly past the upper. It has one continuous dorsal fin, with soft and spiny portions that are roughly the same height, and a similar anal fin below. The pectoral fins are large and rounded, the pelvic fins are fairly small and pointed, and its caudal fin is wide and broom-like; in adults the final rays are typically elongated. The scamp has a slightly elongated, oblong body shape, and is compressed horizontally. It grows fairly large, over 3 feet and almost 30 pounds, but those found in the Bay are usually only 1-2 inches.

Similar Species: The snowy grouper (*Epinephalus niveatus*) and the black grouper (*Mycteroperca bonaci*) are two related species occasionally found in the Bay. The snowy grouper has a deeper body than the scamp, and is predominantly black, sometimes with white spots), except for its tail which is transparent or yellow. The black grouper is darker brown in color, and has black rectangular markings arranged in horizontal lines along its sides.

Range: Outside of Narragansett Bay the scamp is found from Massachusetts to Venezuela, plus the Gulf of Mexico and Caribbean.

Behavior: The scamp, like all other groupers, is a powerful predator that feeds on a wide variety of crabs, lobsters, squids, and fish. Juveniles are potentially vulnerable to predatory fish such as snappers, jacks, striped bass, and summer flounder, while adults are only vulnerable to sharks and other larger groupers. The scamp is a solitary species that spends most of its time cruising above the bottom or resting in holes in the reef. It is a versatile predator, and will either wait in a hole for something to pass by, or actively patrol the reef and sneak up on unsuspecting prey. Adult scamp tend to live in relatively deep water, over rocky bottoms and coral reefs between 80 and 300 feet. The juveniles found in the Bay are typically found hiding in rocky areas, under ledges and amongst aquatic vegetation. Like their close relative, the black sea bass, most scamp are protogynous hermaphrodites, beginning their lives as females and eventually transforming into males. They spawn from May until August, and can be found in the Bay from July until September.

Relationship to People: The scamp is widely considered to be the best eating of all the Atlantic groupers, a family already esteemed as some of the finest food fish. Unsurprisingly, a significant commercial and recreational fishery for this species exists in the South Atlantic and Gulf states. Fortunately, the stock is managed well, and has not been overfished.

How to Find It: The scamp is fairly rare in Narragansett Bay, and also somewhat difficult to catch. Like the spotfin butterflyfish, it is typically found in rocky areas, so seines usually don't work, (although they do sometimes show up in eelgrass beds or among seaweed). The best method is to snorkel with a slurp gun or hand net, although they are very fast and hard to corner.

Miscellaneous Tropicals

Red Goatfish -*Mullus auratus*

Other Names-goatfish, northern goatfish, red mullet, surmullet, golden surmullet

Habitat: It is typically found over sand or mud bottoms in protected bays or harbors. In the beginning of the summer they are found near shore in relatively shallow water, but as the season progresses they move to deeper water.

Description: The red goatfish is certainly one of the most beautifully marked fish, native or tropical, found in Narragansett Bay. Its overall color is an iridescent bluish-silver, brilliantly painted with irregular, bright scarlet blotches, and interlaced with three or four horizontal, electric yellow stripes. Its fins are a dusky brown color, speckled with light spots and stripes, and its eyes are an intense ruby red color. The goatfish has a fairly steep head profile, a small forward-facing mouth, and two long chin barbels arranged in a "v" shape beneath its mouth. It has two similarly-sized triangular dorsal fins, one spiny and one soft, and a smaller triangular anal fin. Its pelvic fins are roughly the same size as its anal fin, its pectoral fins are pointed, and it has a moderately forked caudal fin. The goatfish has an elongated, stocky, and robust body shape which tapers towards its caudal fin. The goatfish is one of the larger tropical strays found in the Bay, and can be up to 4 inches long; adult fish can grow to 10 inches long.

Range: Outside of Narragansett Bay the red goatfish can be found from Nova Scotia to Guyana, including the Gulf of Mexico and much of the Caribbean Sea.

Behavior: The red goatfish is, in many respects, the "kingfish of the tropics." It feeds on benthic invertebrates such as bivalves, shrimps, crabs, polychaete worms, brittle stars, and urchins. The goatfish's predators include large reef fish such as sharks, groupers, snappers, jacks, and small tunas; in Narragansett Bay they are probably vulnerable to species like the striped bass and summer flounder. The goatfish is a fairly active, mostly solitary fish that spends much of its time cruising over the ocean floor in search of prey. It feeds by swimming above the bottom with its barbels extended, and skimming the substratum to detect signs of prey buried just beneath the sand. Several species of Western-Atlantic goatfish, (likely including the red goatfish), exhibit a unique commensal relationship with other reef fish known as "following behavior." This refers to when smaller unrelated species, such as jacks, wrasses, and grunts, will follow a feeding goatfish, and pick off any small creatures released in the sediment that it stirs up.

The red goatfish is found in protected water over sand and mud bottoms. It arrives in the Bay starting in early July, moves to deep waters by late August, and remains there until early October.

Relationship to People: Like the kingfish, the red goatfish makes fine table fare, and is a local delicacy prized in many tropical locales, where they support minor commercial and recreational fisheries. In the Bay, the red goatfish's interesting feeding habits, alluring aesthetic beauty, and relative scarcity make it one of the ultimate prizes for tropical fish collectors.

How to Find It: The red goatfish is one of the rarer species of tropical strays, fortunately, a few are still caught each year. Unlike other tropicals it's not typically associated with eelgrass beds, rather it prefers areas over sand or mud bottoms. It is also one of the earliest tropicals to arrive here, appearing first in July and moving deeper by late August, (ironically when most collectors first start targeting tropicals). Red goatfish are most easily caught by seining.

Miscellaneous Tropicals
Inshore Lizardfish -*Synodus foetens*
Other Names-lizardfish, snakefish, galliwasp, lagarto, sand pike, chile

Habitat: It is almost always found over soft and sandy bottoms, close to shore, in protected bays and sounds.

Description: The inshore lizardfish is a light olive brown color above, fading to a creamy white belly below, with a bluish green cast that develops as individuals mature. On top of this coloration, the lizardfish has several darker blotches over much of its body, including 8 distinctive diamond-shaped markings running along its lateral line. Juveniles also have a series of 13 small black spots along the base of the anal fin. It has large eyes that point upward, a depressed triangular head (when viewed from above), and very large jaws, filled with rows of tiny needlelike teeth. It has a medium sized triangular dorsal fin located midway along its body, and a tiny adipose fin located farther back near its moderately forked caudal fin. It has a large tapering anal fin, rounded pectoral fins, and distinctively large, rounded pelvic fins. The inshore lizardfish's overall body shape is extremely elongate, and cylindrical, tapering slightly towards the caudal fin. Its maximum size is 18 inches, however in the Bay it is usually just 2 to 6 inches.

Range: Outside of Narragansett Bay the inshore lizardfish is found from Massachusetts to Brazil, including the Gulf of Mexico and the Caribbean Sea.

Behavior: The inshore lizardfish is a surprisingly voracious predator, consuming squid, shrimp, and a host of small fish species including anchovies, goatfish, young flounder, and even small jacks. Their relatively small size means that they are at risk from a variety of predators such as sharks, large jacks, snappers, and groupers; the juveniles found in the Bay are likely eaten by fish such as summer flounder and striped bass. The inshore lizardfish is a completely solitary fish, and spends most of its time lying motionless on the bottom waiting to ambush prey. Often times, to aid in its camouflage, it will partially bury itself in the sand, making it even less noticeable to predator and prey alike. When an unsuspecting fish does pass by, the lizardfish will rush out from its hiding place, seize the fish in its spiky jaws, and proceed to swallow it whole. It is incredibly opportunistic, targeting both benthic and pelagic species, and will sometimes attack species too large to actually swallow. The inshore lizardfish lurks in relatively shallow water over sandy or soft bottoms. It is found in the Bay starting in mid-August and remains here until late September.

Relationship to People: Thanks to its small size, voracious appetite, and elongated body lacking in meat, the inshore lizardfish is viewed as a nuisance and pest by both commercial and recreational fisherman. In fact, they are so voracious that in 2006, when lizardfish showed up in Rhode Island in record high numbers, many fisheries experts were concerned they would decimate populations of local species.

How to Find It: Fortunately for most people, inshore lizardfish have not appeared in 2006 numbers for the past several years. But for those who *do* want to catch lizardfish, this means they are now difficult to find, although some are always caught each year. The best time to look for them is at the end of the summer, around the last week of August. The best places are protected sandy beaches near the mouth of the Bay, and the best way to catch them is by seining.

Miscellaneous Tropicals
Bluespotted Cornetfish - *Fistularia tabacaria*
Other Names-cornetfish, trumpet-fish, spotted pipefish, flutemouth

Habitat: It is usually found in shallow eelgrass beds, and over soft bottoms, often in the vicinity of shallow rocky reefs.

Description: The bluespotted cornetfish is an overall olive green to light brown color above, fading to a silvery white below. On top of this base color it has several large azure spots arranged in horizontal rows along the length of its body. The cornetfish is easily distinguished by its elongated, tube-like head and snout, which together occupy more than a third of its total body length. Its small mouth is situated at the tip of its snout, and its eyes are fairly large. It has small rounded pectoral fins, and very small (often indiscernible) pelvic fins. The cornetfish has one small, triangular dorsal fin located far back on its body, mirrored below, almost exactly, by a similarly-sized and shaped anal fin. It has a characteristically unique caudal fin, which is deeply forked and intersected by an elongated caudal whip, (which is actually just one greatly extended middle filament of the fin). The cornetfish is rather large for a tropical stray; adults can grow over 6 feet long, and the strays can be up to 16 inches long.

Range: Outside of Narragansett Bay the cornetfish is found from southern Canada to Brazil, including the Gulf of Mexico and Caribbean Sea. It is also found in the Eastern Atlantic from Cape Verde to Angola.

Behavior: The bluespotted cornetfish, despite its odd appearance, is a skilled predator, which feeds on shrimp, other small invertebrates, and a variety of baitfish, such as mummichogs, anchovies, and silversides. Like most tropical species, in their native range they are vulnerable to predation by any large carnivorous reef fish, such as jacks, snappers, groupers, etc.; in Rhode Island they are likely eaten by species such as striped bass and bluefish. The cornetfish is a sly, solitary hunter that moves slowly yet deliberately, hiding in the shadows, amongst blades of eelgrass, like a snake waiting for prey. Although it may appear slow and awkward, it is actually quite agile, and capable of great bursts of speed when threatened or pursuing a meal. When an unsuspecting fish passes by, the cornetfish rushes up to it and quickly opens its mouth to create a vast suction, which allows it to inhale its prey whole. Young cornetfish typically live in the sheltered waters of eelgrass beds, however as they get larger, they move towards mo open areas, often congregating around t largest rock or object in a given area. Th are found in the Bay from early August un late September.

Relationship to People: Becau of its rather thin, elongated body, and rel tive scarcity, the bluespotted cornetfi holds no economic value to commercial fis erman, and is generally viewed as an oddi by recreational fisherman. Since it can gro over six feet, and has specific feeding r quirements, the cornetfish is nearly imposs ble to keep for all but the most advanced m rine aquarists.

How to Find It: The bluespotted co netfish is very cyclical in terms of abu dance; some years only one or two may b found, other years they are practically ple tiful. They are found in the Bay at the san time as most other tropicals, from August September, and like many other tropica their preferred locale is eelgrass beds. Co sequently, the most efficient way to targ them is with a seine net.

Miscellaneous Tropicals

Northern Sennet - *Sphyraena borealis*
Other Names - sennet, northern barracuda, barracuda

Habitat: It is typically found in shallow eelgrass beds and adjacent sandy or rocky areas. It also sometimes enters saltwater creeks and estuaries.

Description: The northern sennet is a brownish olive-green color above, fading to silver on its sides, with a creamy white belly. On top of this base color, juveniles have variable dark brown mottling which slowly fades to a pure silver color as individuals grow larger. It has very large eyes, and a long, pointed snout. The sennet has a large mouth filled with sharp teeth, and a distinct fleshy-tipped lower jaw that extends past the upper. It has a triangular spiny dorsal fin located in the middle of its body and a triangular soft dorsal fin located roughly halfway between the spiny dorsal and caudal fin. The spiny dorsal fin is reflected below by slightly smaller pelvic fins, and the soft dorsal is mirrored by a similarly sized anal fin. The northern sennet has oblong pectoral fins and a moderately forked caudal fin. Its body shape is slender, elongate, and semi-cylindrical. Adult sennet can grow to about 18 inches long, and the strays are usually between 4 and 8 inches long.

Range: Outside of Narragansett Bay the northern sennet can be found from Massachusetts to South Florida, including much of the Gulf of Mexico.

Behavior: The northern sennet, much like its larger, better-known relative the great barracuda (*Sphyraena barracuda*) is a skilled, efficient predator, albeit in a smaller package. It is almost exclusively a fish-eater, targeting silversides, anchovies, menhaden, and a host of other pelagic species. Due to its small size, (especially compared to the great barracuda, which has few natural predators), the northern sennet is potential prey for large fast-moving fish such as jacks, snook, tuna, or bluefish. Most species have trouble catching northern sennet, however, since they can swim extremely fast. This speed also proves useful while hunting, when the sennet needs to run down potential prey. However it does not waste its energy carelessly chasing after prey, rather it waits patiently in the middle of the water column before striking. Although it is usually a solitary hunter, northern sennet will sometimes work together in small groups to coordinate attacks on large schools of baitfish. It is found close to shore, typically in and around eelgrass beds, but sometimes in saltwater creeks and estuaries as well. It is one of the earliest arriving tropical strays, and can be found from late June to late September.

Relationship to People: The northern sennet is neither large enough nor common enough anywhere in its range to support any major commercial or recreational fishery. When they are encountered they are typically viewed as unique curiosities. They also don't do well in captivity, and so unlike most other tropical strays, they aren't suited for an amateur's aquarium.

How to Find It: The northern sennet is probably the most common tropical stray found in Narragansett Bay. It can be consistently caught every year, starting in late June all the way through until late September. They are most common in the eelgrass beds near the mouth of the Bay. The northern sennet can be caught using a large seine net (the easiest method) or by light tackle angling with small artificial lures. It can also be observed by quietly snorkeling along the edge of eelgrass beds.

Miscellaneous Tropicals

Cobia - *Rachycentron canadum*

Other Names-crab eater, ling, cobbeo, lemonfish, slob

Habitat: It is a roamer, and can show up anywhere from shallow weedy bays, to deep channels over sandy bottoms, and is often associated with buoys and other floating shelter.

Description: Juvenile cobia are easily distinguished from other Narragansett Bay species by their striking, jet-black coloration, overlaid with 1 or 2 white or gold stripes. As they grow larger, cobia lighten in color to a rusty brown above and creamy white below. Its skin is rough and leathery, like that of a shark. The cobia has a broad, flattened head, with a large, terminal mouth, and a slightly protruding lower jaw. Its first dorsal fin is a series of 7-9 disconnected spines, and its soft dorsal fin is long and tapering. Its anal fin is similar to the dorsal fin, but slightly smaller, and its pectoral fins are large and triangular. Juvenile cobia have rounded, fan-like caudal fins, but as they grow larger their caudal fins become forked. The cobia has a sleek, torpedo-like body, and when viewed from a boat it is often mistaken for a small shark. In the Bay, cobia can be anywhere from a few inches long, and less than a pound, to nearly 4 feet and 40 pounds. Farther south they are known to reach over 6 feet long and 170 pounds.

Range: Outside of Narragansett Bay the cobia is found from Massachusetts to Argentina, as well as other tropical and subtropical waters worldwide, except the eastern Pacific.

Behavior: The cobia is a powerful, voracious predator that readily feeds on a wide variety of fish, squid, shrimp, and especially crabs. And although it is a capable predator itself, the cobia will often follow large sharks, rays, and turtles, to feed on anything left in their wake. Cobia are not common prey for most species, even young ones, as they grow extremely fast, and soon become too large for most predators to handle. Still, juveniles occasionally fall prey to species like striped bass, tunas, and dolphinfish, and adults are sometimes targeted by large pelagic sharks, such as shortfin makos. The cobia is a pelagic species, and can show up anywhere from an offshore oil platform to the shallow, grassy flats of an inshore bay. In open water, they tend to congregate around floating objects such as boats, navigation markers, mats of seaweed, and anything else that provides cover. It is a predominantly solitary hunter (although it sometimes travels in small groups), and can be seen both basking at the surface and roaming deep near the bottom. Cobia undergo northerly migrations across the Eastern seaboard, arriving in the Bay in late summer and leaving by mid-autumn.

Relationship to People: The cobia is a popular species amongst recreation fisherman because of its large size and rugged fighting abilities. The cobia is also a delicious food fish, with a unique taste unlike most species. They are often caught incidentally by commercial fisherman, but the itinerant lifestyles make them difficult to target. Cobia aquaculture is already well established in certain parts of the world, especially East Asia, and recent projects in the US aim to follow suit.

How to Find It: The cobia is fairly rare in Narragansett Bay, although warming waters are bringing more into the Bay every summer. Juveniles can be caught by seining. The best places to look are protected coves although it is difficult to predict exactly where they will show up. Adults are occasionally caught while bottom fishing for species like fluke and sea bass.

Tropical Baitfish

Silver Jenny -*Eucinostomus gula*
Other Names-jenny mojarra, common mojarra

Habitat: It is found in protected estuaries over sand and mud bottoms, often amongst eelgrass and other aquatic vegetation.

Description: The silver jenny is, as its name suggests, a silvery-white color overall, although young fish often have a series of darker diagonal blotches and bars, which fade as they grow larger. It has dusky-brown fins, and a spiny dorsal fin tipped in black. Its snout is often darker as well, especially in juveniles. The silver jenny has a very distinct, nearly triangular head, with a pointed snout, a set of small protrusible jaws, and very large eyes. It has one continuous dorsal fin, with a triangular spiny section, and a rectangular soft section. Its anal fin is about the same size and shape as the soft section of its dorsal fin, its pelvic fins are small, its pectoral fins are pointed, and it has a moderately forked caudal fin. The silver jenny's overall body shape is deep and somewhat oblong, with a slightly arched back. Silver jennies are fairly small fish, growing only to 9 inches long, although in the Bay they rarely grow larger than an inch.

Range: Outside of Narragansett Bay the silver jenny is found from Massachusetts to Argentina, including the Gulf of Mexico and the Caribbean Sea.

Behavior: The silver jenny's diet is limited by the size of its mouth to benthic invertebrates such as bivalves, polychaete worms, ostracods, and amphipods. In the southern part of its range, it is an important food source for several kinds of predatory fish, such as groupers, snappers and drums. Here in Narragansett Bay, they are so small that nearly any predator larger than them is a potential threat. The silver jenny is an active species typically found in small schools. These schools both protect against predators and facilitate efficient foraging strategies. The silver jenny tends to feed in the morning and uses its sense of sight to actively search for signs of prey hiding on the ocean floor. Once it has discovered something, the silver jenny tilts its body at a forty five degree angle, sticks its protrusible snout into the ocean bottom, and slurps up a mouthful of invertebrates, as well as sediment which it then expels through its gills. As its diet suggests, the silver jenny is found over sand and mud bottoms, usually in protected areas such as bays or estuaries; it is also associated with aquatic vegetation, especially seagrass beds. The silver jenny is found in the Bay from August to early October. Farther south, adults spawn year round, although peak mating occurs during the summer months.

Relationship to People: In the Southern and Gulf States, the silver jenny supports a minor commercial and recreational fishery as bait for game species such as snook and red drum, although large jennies themselves also taste quite good. In the Bay, the only use for silver jennies would be in marine aquaria, and even so they don't look particularly interesting.

How to Find It: The silver jenny is one of the rarer tropical strays found in the Bay. Only a few are caught every couple of years, and so they are fairly difficult to target. The best chance for someone intent on finding a silver jenny, is to search near the mouth of the Bay off protected sandy beaches, ideally those with eelgrass beds or other aquatic vegetation. They could presumably be caught with traps, hand nets, and cast nets, but, as is often the case, a seine net is the most effective.

Tropical Baitfish

White Mullet - *Mugil curema*

Other Names - mullet, silver mullet, lisa blanca, liseta

Habitat: It is always found in shallow water, often in the margins right along the coastline. It is usually found over muddy or sandy bottoms, often in protected salt ponds, brackish water, or amongst aquatic vegetation.

Description: The white mullet is best described (in terms of appearance) as a combination between an alewife and a killifish. Overall it is a shiny silver color, with a bluish green tinge above, (like an alewife). Its fins are typically a dusky brown color, its gill flaps have dark blue and yellowish-bronze markings, and it has a dark blue spot at the base of each pectoral fin. The white mullet has a distinctively flat head, a blunt nose, a small mouth, and comparatively large eyes. It has one triangular spiny dorsal fin located midway along its body, and a similarly shaped soft dorsal fin located farther back, reflected directed below by a slightly larger anal fin. It has fairly large pelvic fins, a moderately forked caudal fin, and pectoral fins situated high on its body. Its body shape is elongated, cylindrical, and semi compressed (like a killifish). It can grow as large as 15 inches long in certain places, but in the Bay it is usually between 2 and 4 inches long.

Range: Outside of Narragansett Bay the white mullet can be found from New England to Southern Brazil. It is also present in parts of the eastern Atlantic and Pacific Oceans.

Behavior: The white mullet is one of only a few fish species in the Bay that is primarily herbivorous. Juveniles hunt near the surface, and feed predominantly on plankton, but as they grow larger, they adopt a benthic foraging style, and consume detritus, algae, diatoms, and fine sediment particles. Farther south, where it is common, the white mullet is prey for a variety of species, including bottlenose dolphins, cormorants, wading birds, spotted sea trout, red drum, etc.; in the Bay it is at risk from birds and large predatory fish. Fortunately, the mullet has several tricks to maximize its chances for survival. Mullet tend to stick together in small tight schools, they often inhabit secluded shallow bays inaccessible to many predators, and, when necessary, they are skilled jumpers. In fact, schools of mullet can often be seen jumping in unison to escape an approaching predator. This jumping behavior also serves an additional purpose, considering the low oxygen environments this species calls home. Thanks to a modified swim bladder, mullet have the ability to process atmospheric oxygen, which they intake by either gulping at the surface or by jumping through the air. Mullet can be found in the Bay starting in late July, but are most common around the first full moon of September.

Relationship to People: Although it is not as economically important as large mullet species, the white mullet does support a significant commercial fishery in the southern part of its range. Not only does have delicious flesh, but its roe is tasty well. It is also often used by recreation fishermen as bait for prized game species such as sea trout and snook.

How to Find It: The white mullet is fairly regular seasonal visitor to Narragansett Bay. In fact, some fisherman consider its a rival the beginning of the fall fishing season. The best time to look for them is in mid-September after the first full moon. White mullet are usually found among aquatic vegetation in protected bays, estuaries, or salt ponds. They can be caught with cast nets, seine nets, or hand nets.

Part 3: Supplemental Photos

Top Left: the wide, gaping mouth of a striped bass; Top Right: the steep head profile of a scup, showing iridescent purple coloration; Bottom Left: the large head of a mature male black sea bass, showing the beginnings of a distinctive head hump.

Top Left: the white chin and human-like teeth of a tautog; Top right: the large, toothy mouth of a summer flounder, showing mottled camouflage coloration; Bottom: the uniquely-shaped caudal fin of a northern kingfish.

Top: the underside of a clearnose skate, showing its distinctive "clear nose"; Bottom Left: top view of an oyster toadfish showing tadpole-like body shape; Bottom Right: top view of northern puffer, showing box-like body shape.

Top: the spiky jaws of an Atlantic needlefish; Middle Left: the parrot-like teeth of a northern puffer; Middle Right: the bizarre horse-like head of a lined seahorse, showing many fleshy protuberances; Bottom: the bright mating coloration of a common mummichog.

Top: the midsection of a rainwater killifish showing a distinctive dark cross-hatch pattern; Bottom: the dusky black and lime-green color stages of the American eel.

Top: an upper view of an inshore lizardfish, showing large pelvic fins and upward-pointing eyes; Middle Left: the head of a red goatfish, showing two long chin barbels; Middle Right: the head of a northern sennet, showing its extended lower jaw and pointed teeth; Bottom: an upper view of a bluespotted cornetfish.

Top: an American eel found over 200 miles from the Atlantic Ocean in Pennsylvania's Delaware River; Middle: an Atlantic needlefish in the shallow waters of the Florida Keys; Bottom: an adult trunkfish in its normal range: the warm waters of the Caribbean Sea.

Top: a group of bluefish orchestrate a coordinated attack on a school of anchovies and menhaden; Bottom: a summer flounder lies partially buried in sand, waiting for prey to pass by.

Top: a northern searobin searches for food along a sandy bottom by using its modified pectoral fins to detect prey buried in the substrate; Bottom: a foraging goatfish is followed by a tropical wrasse feeding on the small marine organisms it stirs up.

Top: a small scup devoured by seabirds; Bottom Left: two humpback whales feeding on American sand lances off the coast of Massachusetts; Bottom Right: a snowy egret stalking killifish and alewives in a salt marsh

Top: a winter flounder well camouflaged against a sandy bottom; Bottom Left: a large school of anchovies takes shelter in the rocky shallows; Bottom Right: a frightened puffer inflates itself to protect against predators.

Top: a small hogchoker lies motionless on the sandy bottom of a tea-colored brackish stream; Bottom: a small band of striped killifish explores the edges of a salt marsh during high tide.

Top: A large, writhing mass of Atlantic silversides spawns in the shallow margins of a salt marsh; Bottom: the recently hatched egg case or "mermaid's purse" of a little skate.

Top: a fisherman takes one more cast before the arrival of an approaching storm; Bottom: an old man fishes for tautog from a slippery rock edge.

Top: a group of surfcasters wait for the next striped bass to bite; Bottom: a striped bass stubbornly resists at the end of an angler's line.

Top: a juvenile bluefish caught from shore on a "snapper" rig; Bottom: an adult bluefish caught trolling with a bucktail.

Top Left: after a morning of successful fishing, a recreational angler fillets a tautog on the trip back to port; Top Right: scup travel together in schools and are sometimes caught simultaneously on double-rigs; Bottom: considered "trash fish" by some anglers, northern searobins are sometimes cruelly left on shore to die.

Top: a student researcher from the University of Rhode Island waits to retrieve an otter trawl; Bottom: a fisheries scientist sorts through a recently trawled catch of skate, scup, sea-robin, and other bottom fish.

Top: a scientist from Roger Williams University examines a recently caught smooth dogfish; Bottom: researchers observe a hake via live-streaming ROV feed at the Inner Space Center of URI's Graduate School of Oceanography.

Top: a tautog tagged by the American Littoral Society; Bottom: a scientist from the University of Rhode Island shows a group of students a little skate's egg case.

References

2014 Sector Management Plan for the Finfish Fishery. State of Rhode Island and Providence Plantations Department of Environmental Management, Division of Fish and Wildlife Marine Fisheries. 2013. Web.

Adams, Aaron J., et al. "Patterns of juvenile habitat use and seasonality of settlement by permit, *Trachinotus falcatus*." *Environmental biology of fishes* 75.2 (2006): 209-217. 2006. Web.

Alden, Peter. *National Audubon Society field guide to New England.* New York: Knopf, 1998. Print.

American eel: Anguilla rostrata. Washington D.C.: U.S. Fish and Wildlife Service, 2011. Web.

Annual Report of the New Jersey State Museum. Trenton, NJ: New Jersey State Museum, MacCrellish & Quigley State Printers, 1905. Web.

Ayala-Pérez, L. A., J. Campos, and M. Tapia-García. "Distribution, abundance and population parameters of silver perch "*Bairdiella chryosura*"(Lacepede, 1802)(Pisces: Scianidae) in Terminos lagoon, Campeche, Mexico." *Thalassas: An international journal of marine sciences 22.1* (2006): 9-18. 2006. Web.

Bean, Tarleton H. *Catalogue of the Fishes of New York.* Albany, NY: New York State Museum, Bulletin 60, Zoology 9, 1903. Web

Bester, Cathleen. "Cobia." Gainesville, FL: Florida Museum of Natural History. Web.

Bigelow, H.B., and W.C. Schroeder. *Fishes of the Gulf of Maine.* Washington, D.C.: U.S. Fish and Wildlife Service, Fishery Bulletin 74, Vol. 53, 1953. Print.

"Bluespotted Cornetfish, Fistularia commersonii." RedOrbit.com, Fish Reference Library, 2014. Web.

Bondorew, Ray. "Mullet Moon: The Finer Points of Finding and Imitating Mullet." Reel-Time, 1996. Web.

Bourque, Gene, et al. *Fishing New England: a Rhode Island shore guide.* Falmouth, MA: On The Water, 2001. Print.

Caldwell, David Keller. *Development and Distribution of the Short Bigeye. Pseudopriacanthus Altus (Gill) in the Western North Atlantic.* US Fish and Wildlife Service, 1962. Web.

Casey, John G. *Angler's Guide to Sharks of the Northeastern United States: Maine to Chesapeake Bay.* Washington D.C.: U.S. Fish and Wildlife Service, Bureau of Sport Fisheries and Wildlife, Circular No. 179, 1964. Print.

Chao, L.N. and J.A. Musick. *Life history, feeding habits, and functional morphology of juvenile sciaenid fishes in the York River Estuary, Virginia.* US National Marine Fisheries Service, Fishery Bulletin 75: 657-702. 1977. Web.

Claro, Rodolfo, Kenyon C. Lindeman, and Lynne R. Parenti. *Ecology of the marine fishes of Cuba.* Washington D.C: Smithsonian Institution Press, 2001. Print.

Class Osteichthyes. Smithsonian Institute, Smithsonian Marine Station at Fort Pierce, 2011. Web.

Cross, Jeffrey N., and Michael P. Fahay. Essential fish habitat source document. Butterfish, Peprilus triacanthus, life history and habitat characteristics. DIANE Publishing, 1999. Web.

Cruz-Escalona, Víctor Hugo, et al. "Feeding habits and trophic morphology of inshore lizardfish (Synodus foetens) on the central continental shelf off Veracruz, Gulf of Mexico." *Journal of Applied Ichthyology* 21.6 (2005): 525-530. 2005. Web.

Curran, Mary C. *Occurrence of tropical fishes in New England waters.* Woods Hole, MA: Woods Hole Oceanographic Institution, 1989. Web.

Dovel, William L., J. A. Mihursky, and Andrew J. McErlean. "Life history aspects of the hogchoker, Trinectes maculatus, in the Patuxent River estuary, Maryland." *Chesapeake Science* 10.2 (1969): 104-119. Web.

Dunaway, Vic, and Eric Wickstrom. *Sport fish of the Atlantic.* Miami, FL: Florida Sportsman, 2003. Print.

Dunaway, Vic, and Kevin R. Brant. *Sport fish of the Gulf of Mexico.* Miami, FL: Florida Sportsman, 2000. Print.

Easley, Kenneth. "Tropical Fish of Rhode Island." Kingston, RI: University of Rhode Island, 1999. PowerPoint Presentation.

Filer, Kelly. "The Elusive Barrelfish: An Enigma Wrapped in a Mystery." Washington D.C.: NOAA Office of Ocean Exploration and Research, 2012. Web.

"FishWatch." Washington D.C.: NOAA Fisheries. Web.

Forbes, Donna M. *Save the Bay's uncommon guide to common life of Narragansett Bay and Rhode Island waters.* Providence, R.I: Save the Bay, 2008. Print.

Foster, Susan A. "Understanding the evolution of behavior in threespine stickleback: the value of geographic variation." *Behaviour* (1995): 1107-1129. Web.

Froese, R. and D. Pauly. *FishBase*. Fishbase.org, 2013. Web.

Gilbert, Carter R., and James D. Williams. *National Audubon Society field guide to fishes.* New York: Alfred A. Knopf, 2002. Print.

Gordon, Bernard L. *A guide book to the marine fishes of Rhode Island.* Watch Hill, RI: Book & Tackle Shop, 1974. Print.

Guénette, Sylvie, and Ronald L. Hill. "A trophic model of the coral reef ecosystem of La Parguera, Puerto Rico: synthesizing fisheries and ecological data." *Caribbean Journal of Science* 45.2-3 (2009): 317-337. 2009. Web.

Hall, Mark. "Marine Life Series: Tropical Strays, A Photo Essay." Kos Media LLC, Daily Kos, 2006. Web.

Hassan-Williams, Carla and Timothy H. Bonner. "Mugil Curema-White Mullet." Texas State University-San Marcos, Texas A&M Press, 2007. Web.

"Information from FAO Species Identification Guide Western Central Atlantic: Atlantic moonfish - Selene setapinnis." The College of William and Mary, Virginia Institute of Marine Science, 2014. Web.

Kalmanzon, Eliahu, et al. "Receptor-mediated toxicity of pahutoxin, a marine trunkfish surfactant." *Toxicon* 42.1 (2003): 63-71.

Kendall, William C. Fauna of New England: List of the Pisces, Volume 8. Boston, MA: Boston Society of Natural History, Gurdon Saltonstall Fund, 1908. Web.

Lazzari, M. A., K. W. Able, and M. P. Fahay. "Life history and food habits of the grubby, Myoxocephalus aeneus (Cottidae), in a Cape Cod estuary." *Copeia* (1989): 7-12. Web.

"Lookdown-Chesapeake Bay Program." Annapolis, MD: Chesapeake Bay Program, 2012. Web.

Maddalena, Alessandro, and Walter Heim. *Sharks of New England.* Camden, ME: Down East Books, 2010. Print.

Monti, Dave. "Local angler catches a cobia…an exotic fish." *Warwick Beacon.* 10 July 2013. Web.

Moss, Sandford A. "The responses of planehead filefish, Monocanthus hispidis (Linnaeus), to low temperature." *Chesapeake Science* 14.4 (1973): 300-303. Web.

Munro, J. L. *Caribbean coral reef fishery resources.* Manila, Philippines: International Center for Living Aquatic Resources Management, 1983. Print.

Nichols, J.T. and C.M. Breder. *The Marine Fishes of New York and Southern New England.* New York: New York Zoological Society, 1927. Print.

Pompano and Permit: Quick, Silver Duo. St. Petersburg, FL: Florida Fish and Wildlife Conservation Commission, Fish and Wildlife Research Institute, 2005. Web.

Poulos-Boggis, Ned. "Mullet Mini Report." Sarasota, FL: New College of Florida, Marine Science Outreach Initiative, 2007. Web.

Price, Kent S. "Copulatory behavior in the clearnose skate, Raja eglanteria, in lower Chesapeake Bay." *Copeia* (1967): 854-855. Web.

Richards, C. E., and M. Castagna. "Distribution, growth, and predation of juvenile white mullet (Mugil curema) in oceanside waters of Virginia's eastern shore." *Chesapeake Science* 17.4 (1976): 308-309. 1976. Web.

Robins, C R., et al. *A field guide to Atlantic Coast fishes of North America.* Boston: Houghton Mifflin, 1986. Print.

Rocha, L., McGovern, J.C., Craig, M.T., Choat, J.H., Ferreira, B., Bertoncini, A.A. & Craig, M. 2008. *Mycteroperca phenax*. The IUCN Red List of Threatened Species. Web.

Ross, Michael R., and Robert C. Biagi. *Recreational fisheries of coastal New England.* Amherst, Mass: University of Massachusetts Press, 1991. Print.

Roux, Olivier, and François Conand. "Feeding habits of the bigeye scad, *Selar crumenophthalmus* (Carangidae), in la réunion island waters (south-western Indian Ocean)." *Cybium* 24.2 (2000): 173-179. 2000. Web.

Rowland, William J. "Reproductive behavior of the fourspine stickleback, Apeltes quadracus." *Copeia* (1974): 183-194. Web.

Sazima, C., et al. "The goatfish *Pseudupeneus maculatus* and its follower fishes at an oceanic island in the tropical west Atlantic." *Journal of Fish Biology* 69.3 (2006): 883-891. 2006. Web.

Schwartz, Frank J. "Biology of the striped cusk-eel, *Ophidion marginatum*, from North Carolina." *Bulletin of marine science* 61.2 (1997): 327-342. 1997. Web.

Schwartz, Frank J. "The barrelfish from Chesapeake Bay and the Middle Atlantic bight, with comments on its zoogeography." *Chesapeake Science* 4.3 (1963): 147-149. Web.

Shingles, A., et al. "Reflex Cardioventilatory Responses to Hypoxia in the Flathead Gray Mullet (Mugil cephalus) and Their Behavioral Modulation by Perceived Threat of Predation and Water Turbidity*." *Physiological and Biochemical Zoology* 78.5 (2005): 744-755. 2005. Web.

Smith, C L. *National Audubon Society field guide to tropical marine fishes of the Caribbean, the Gulf of Mexico, Florida, the Bahamas, and Bermuda.* New York: Alfred A. Knopf, 1997. Print

Sosebee, Kathy. "Status of Fishery Resources off the Northeastern US." Washington D.C.: NOAA Northeast Fisheries Science Center, 2006. Web.

Steimle, Frank W. *Essential fish habitat source document. Scup, Stenotomus chrysops, life history and habitat characteristics.* DIANE Publishing, 1999. Web.

Thomson, K.S., W.H. Weed, A.G Taruski, and D.E. Simanek. *Saltwater Fishes of Connecticut.* Hartford, CT: State Geological and Natural History Survey of Connecticut, Bulletin 105, 1978. Print.

Tracy, Henry C. *Annotated List of Fishes Known to Inhabit the Waters of Rhode Island.* Providence, RI: E.L. Freeman Company, 1909. Web.

Watling, Les, et al. *Life between the tides: marine plants and animals of the Northeast.* Gardiner, ME: Tilbury House Publishers, 2003. Print.

Wiggers, Robert. *Crevalle Jack. In: Comprehensive Wildlife Conservation Strategy.* Columbia, SC: South Carolina Department of Natural Resources, 2005. Web.

Wirgin, Isaac, et al. "Mechanistic basis of resistance to PCBs in Atlantic tomcod from the Hudson River." *Science* 331.6022 (2011): 1322-1325. 2011. Web.

Wyanski, David M. *Naked Goby.* Columbia, SC: South Carolina Department of Natural Resources, 2005. Web.

Young, Chip. "Mother Nature's Lizardfish Legerdemain." Providence, RI: Providence Journal, October 10, 2007. Web.

Zahorcsak, P., R. A. M. Silvano, and I. Sazima. "Feeding biology of a guild of benthivorous fishes in a sandy shore on south-eastern Brazilian coast." *Revista Brasileira de Biologia* 60.3 (2000): 511-518. 2000. Web.

Made in the USA
San Bernardino, CA
29 July 2017